The
Recipe
Keeper

The Recipe Keeper

The perfect place to store your favorite recipes, treasured ideas, hints, and tips

First published in 2011
LOVE FOOD is an imprint of Parragon Books Ltd

Parragon
Queen Street House
4 Queen Street
Bath BA1 1HE, UK

ISBN: 978-1-4454-3961-7

Printed in China

Edited by Fiona Biggs
Additional photography and styling by Mike Cooper
Additional home economy by Lincoln Jefferson
Internal design by Sarah Knight

Notes for the Reader
This book uses imperial, metric, and US cup measurements. Follow the same units of measurement throughout; do not mix imperial and metric. All spoon measurements are level: teaspoons are assumed to be 5 ml, and tablespoons are assumed to be 15 ml. Unless otherwise stated, milk is assumed to be whole, eggs and individual vegetables such as potatoes are medium, and pepper is freshly ground black pepper. The times given are an approximate guide only. Preparation times differ according to the techniques used by different people and the cooking times may also vary from those given as a result of the type of oven used. Optional ingredients, variations or serving suggestions have not been included in the calculations.

Recipes using raw or very lightly cooked eggs should be avoided by infants, the elderly, pregnant women, convalescents, and anyone with a chronic condition. Pregnant and breastfeeding women are advised to avoid eating peanuts and peanut products. Sufferers from nut allergies should be aware that some of the ready-prepared ingredients used in the recipes in this book may contain nuts. Always check the packaging before use. Vegetarians should be aware that some of the ready-prepared ingredients used in the recipes in this book may contain animal products. Always check the packaging before use.

Picture Acknowledgements
The publisher would like to thank the following for permission to reproduce copyright material:
Cover illustration: Seamless vegetable pattern: vector format © Accent/Shutterstock
Vintage labels © AKaiser/Shutterstock
Close-up notepaper on cork board © Picsfive/Shutterstock
A coffee cup stain © Tyler Olson/Shutterstock
Masking tape © Samantha Grady/Shutterstock
Vintage prints and crockery supplied courtesy of Istock images

Contents

INTRODUCTION

Busy kitchens mean busy cooks, and busy cooks don't always have the time to organize their recipe collection in the way they would like. Magazines, recipe printouts, and scribbled ideas can quickly build up and become unusable, as you struggle to locate that recipe you found months ago that you are now desperate to make! Enter *The Recipe Keeper*, the essential addition to your cookbook collection!

The Recipe Keeper is an easy way to gather together and safely keep recipes torn from magazines, printed from the internet or handwritten with love and passed down through the generations (with splashes and food stains galore). Invaluable pockets are included for storing cherished recipes, and the useful note section lets you quickly jot down and safely keep any food-related tip if the need arises. There is plenty of space for writing in new recipe ideas from friends and family, creating the ultimate kitchen resource that would rival any store-bought cookbook.

Also included is a selection of classic recipes, savory and sweet, that will satisfy any food lover. From family dinners to delicious baked treats, there are recipes for every occasion to impress friends and family. With an extensive introduction that covers all the basic cooking techniques and ingredients, *The Recipe Keeper* is all you need to whip up and dish out the most delicious dishes!

PANTRY ESSENTIALS

A good store of nonperishable foodstuffs is an essential part of any kitchen. Well-stocked cupboards, and perhaps a freezer, will ensure you always have a good selection of staple items on hand for any occasion. Regularly check and discard any stored items that are out of date.

OILS

There are many different varieties of oil available these days, but it is not necessary to buy them all. You simply need oil that is suitable for drizzling and for cooking at high temperatures.

OLIVE OIL

This is mildly fruity oil is ideal for drizzling over salads. It can range from a champagne color to bright green. The best oils are cold-pressed—this is a chemical-free process that uses only pressure and produces a low level of acidity. You can also flavor it with different ingredients. For example, try adding some herbs, such as basil leaves, or some garlic to it—after a day or two the oil will become infused with their flavor. Its smoke point (the temperature at which it begins to smoke) is 410°F/210°C.

EXTRA VIRGIN OLIVE OIL

Produced from the first cold-pressing of the olives, this oil has a very low acid level. It is the most expensive type of olive oil and has a peppery, fruity flavor. You can use it for drizzling over salads and hot dishes, such as pizzas. Its smoke point is 410°F/210°C.

CORN OIL

This is a good choice for cooking. It has a strong, distinctive flavor that makes it unsuitable for dressings and drizzling. Its smoke point is 410°F/210°C.

SUNFLOWER OIL

This is a good multipurpose oil that can be used for most cooking purposes. However, it is not recommended for deep-frying because this method needs an oil with a higher smoke point. Sunflower oil has a very light flavor and is, therefore, ideal in dressings. The smoke point of sunflower oil is 390°F/199°C.

SESAME OIL

This oil is excellent for frying and stir-frying and comes in two varieties: one has a light color and nutty flavor; the other is darker and has a stronger flavor. Its smoke point is 410°F/210°C.

VEGETABLE OIL

A blend of various oils, mainly canola, soybean, coconut, and palm. It is best used for frying instead of in salads because it is very greasy.

SOYBEAN OIL

This economical oil is extracted from soybeans and has a light yellow color. Like canola oil, its popularity is growing because it is low in saturated fat. It has a strong taste and is unsuitable for dressings or drizzling. Its smoke point is 450°F/232°C, which makes it ideal for all types of cooking, including deep-frying.

CANOLA OIL

This oil (made from rapeseeds) is gaining in popularity because it is lower in saturated fat than other oils. It also contains the omega-3 essential fatty acid, which is now widely believed to help reduce cholesterol levels. It has a mild flavor making it suitable for salads.

PEANUT OIL

A combination of a very mild flavor and a high smoke point of 450°F/232°C makes peanut oil very versatile. It is suitable for drizzling, dressings, and mayonnaise as well as all forms of cooking, including deep-frying.

VINEGARS

Vinegar adds a wonderful, pungent kick to dressings, marinades, sauces, and a wide range of dishes. It is available in different varieties, and here are some of the most popular types.

WINE VINEGARS

These are available in different varieties, mainly red, white, and sherry. They can be used in dressings, marinades, and sauces, and can be sprinkled over food.

CIDER VINEGAR

This vinegar is made from apples and has a strong, sharp taste. It is best used with meats and in pickling and making condiments.

MALT VINEGAR

This is made from malted barley and is available as a strong, colorless form used for pickling and as a dark brown type used in condiments.

RICE VINEGAR

Made from fermented rice, this mild, sweet vinegar is often used in Chinese and Japanese cooking.

BALSAMIC VINEGAR

This delicious vinegar is thick, dark, and slightly sweet. It is made from grape juice that is aged in barrels over a period of years.

WHITE VINEGAR

Also called distilled white vinegar, this harsh, sour vinegar is best reserved for pickling.

PASTA, NOODLES & GRAINS

All these different dried pasta shapes, noodles, and grains keep well in the pantry. They are ideal for cooking quick, satisfying meals at short notice.

LONG PASTA

There are different varieties of dried pastas with long shapes, including spaghetti, fettuccine (narrow ribbons), tagliatelle (slightly wider ribbons), and vermicelli (very fine, hairlike lengths). These pastas are usually made with durum wheat or whole wheat flour, and they may be colored by using such ingredients as spinach (green), beet juice (red), tomatoes (orange-red), or even squid ink (black).

SHORT PASTA TYPES

Dried short shapes of pasta include conchiglie (shells), fusilli (spirals), farfalle (bows), and tubular varieties, such as penne and macaroni. These shorter shapes are particularly good for holding chunky sauces.

OTHER SHAPES OF DRIED PASTA

Other favorite shapes to keep in your pantry include lasagna (rectangular noodles) and cannelloni (large tubes).

DRIED NOODLES

Most noodles are associated with Asian cooking. The main difference between noodles and long types of pasta is that noodles usually have egg added, such as Chinese egg noodles. Alternatively, sometimes they are made from rice flour. Noodles are very popular in stir-fries and soups. Some types are prepared so they need no cooking—you simply soak them in hot water for a few minutes before adding them to the dish of your choice.

LONG-GRAIN RICE

You can buy white and brown types of long-grain rice. When cooked, the grains stay dry and separate and do not clump together. This rice is used in savory dishes.

MEDIUM-GRAIN RICE

These grains are a little shorter than long-grain rice and more moist. They tend to clump together when cooked. This rice is used in savory dishes, such as Spanish paella and Japanese sushi.

SHORT-GRAIN RICE

This rice has short grains that are more starchy and moist than medium- and long-grain rice. There are different varieties, including pearl rice and glutinous rice (used in Asian cooking) and arborio rice (used in risottos).

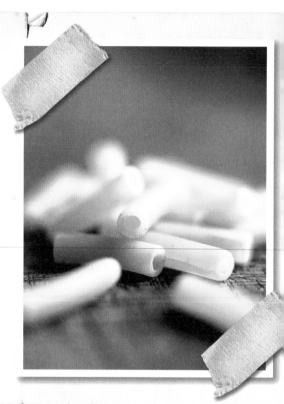

INSTANT RICE

The grains in instant or quick rice are polished and partly boiled so that they are quick and easy to cook and stay fluffy and separate. Although instant rice is a convenient alternative to white or brown rice, it does not have as much flavor.

WILD RICE

This is a marsh grass that is cultivated in the United States and Canada. The grains are long and black and have a nutty flavor. Wild rice is expensive, so for economy reasons it is often mixed with less expensive brown long-grain rice.

BULGUR WHEAT

Wheat kernels that have had the bran removed are steamed, dried, and ground into different degrees of coarseness. The golden-brown grain has a nutty flavor. It can be cooked like rice and is excellent in salads.

COUSCOUS

This is not a true grain, but pieces of semolina coated in a wheat flour. It is a fine side dish for a savory meal.

CORNMEAL

Ground from dried corn kernels, cornmeal is available in fine, medium, and coarse textures and is white, yellow, or blue. The Italian polenta is a coarsely ground version sold in some grocery stores.

DRIED BEANS

All dried beans except lentils and split peas need soaking for at least 8 hours, then boiling rapidly for 10 minutes before cooking for around 45 minutes.

CANNELLINI BEANS

A type of haricot bean, these long, creamy white beans are excellent in soups and salads.

RED KIDNEY BEANS

These red, kidney-shaped beans can be added to soups, salads, stews, and other savory dishes, such as chili con carne. They can cause food poisoning if not boiled rapidly for at least 10 minutes.

ADUKI BEANS

These small red beans are popular in Japanese cooking, especially coated with sugar. They are also good in soups and salads.

LIMA BEANS

These white, kidney-shaped beans are excellent in soups and salads.

SOYBEANS

Although most soybeans are yellow, they can also be black, brown, or green. They are much richer in nutrients than the other dried beans, and are particularly full of protein, as well as iron and calcium. Soybeans are used to make cooking oils and margarine, flour, soy milk and cheeses, soy sauce, tofu, miso, and textured vegetable protein.

CHICKPEAS

These round, beige legumes have a nutty flavor and are excellent in soups, stews, and salads, as well as ground up in dips, such as hummus. They need a longer soaking and cooking time than many other dried beans, so it is good to keep some canned chickpeas on hand for when you have little time.

LENTILS

These tiny, disk-shaped legumes are available in different varieties and colors. Red and orange lentils become mushy when cooked and are, therefore, ideal pureed and used in soups and sauces. The green and brown varieties (including Puy, or French green, lentils) keep their shape when cooked and are ideal in warm winter salads, sauces, stews, and other savory dishes.

SPLIT PEAS

These small peas are disk shaped and split along a natural seam. They can be yellow or green and are excellent cooked and pureed. They are also good in soups, casseroles, and other savory dishes.

BLACK-EYED PEAS

These small beige peas have a circular black "eye." They are commonly found in Chinese cooking and are very popular in sauces, stir-fries, and soups.

BORLOTTI BEANS

These oval-shaped beans have pale pink to maroon streaked skin. They are creamy when cooked and are excellent in soups, dips, and other savory dishes.

NUTS & SEEDS

Nuts and seeds can quickly turn rancid due to their high oil content. Store nuts with shells in a cool, dry place. If shelled, refrigerate in airtight containers.

ALMONDS

These lozenge-shaped nuts have a thin brown covering and a cream center. They come in two types, sweet and bitter, but it is the sweet variety that is normally used. Available whole, blanched, chopped, and candied, they are excellent in both savory and sweet dishes.

HAZELNUTS

These small, round nuts have a brown covering and a cream interior, and a rich, sweet flavor. They are especially popular in cereals and granola, casseroles and other savory dishes, such as nut loaf, and in sweet dishes, including cakes and cookies.

WALNUTS

These nuts have a large, round, wrinkled shell and two double lobes inside. The nuts have a delicious creamy taste and are good in salads and savory dishes, as well as sweet dishes and cakes. They also make a very flavorful oil.

PECANS

These nuts are golden brown with a beige interior. They have a very high fat content and are used in a variety of savory dishes and desserts.

CASHEW NUTS

These creamy, butter-flavored kidney-shaped nuts have a high fat content and are delicious roasted and added to stir-fries and casseroles.

PISTACHIO NUTS

These pale green nuts have a delicate flavor. They are often used in stuffings and also to decorate desserts.

PINE NUTS

These small, oval nuts are excellent toasted or dry-fried.

SAUCES & CONDIMENTS

A good selection of sauces and condiments is invaluable in the kitchen, and will ensure you always have the right ingredients on hand to add exciting and interesting flavors to your dishes.

KETCHUP

This sauce is popular in Western cooking and is a favorite condiment often served with cooked foods, such as hamburgers and french fries. It is also good as an ingredient in dressings and relishes.

STEAK SAUCE

This brown sauce, whether a sweet or tart version, is often used to flavor beef.

SOY SAUCE

This sauce is essential for stir-fries and other Asian dishes. The Chinese version is salty, and the Japanese version is sweeter.

HOISIN SAUCE

This sweet soy-based sauce with a sticky texture is very popular in Chinese cooking. It is known by various names, such as Peking sauce.

WORCESTERSHIRE SAUCE

This strongly flavored sauce is made with onions, molasses, and anchovies, and is used to season meats, gravies, and soups.

PESTO SAUCE

Made from basil, garlic, pine nuts, Parmesan cheese, and olive oil, pesto is good with pasta.

TABASCO SAUCE

This very hot chili sauce is used in dishes to give them a kick, such as Mexican salsas. It is also used to season certain cocktails.

THAI FISH SAUCE (NAM PLA)

This salty sauce is made from fermented fish and has a very strong taste and smell. It is used to flavor Thai dishes and as a table condiment.

OTHER ITEMS

Here is a selection of other items you will find useful to keep in your pantry.

BOUILLON CUBES

These are very convenient for soups, casseroles, and other dishes, particularly if you do not have enough time to make fresh stock.

MISO

This is a paste made from fermented soybeans. It is used in Japanese cooking to thicken and flavor soups and other dishes.

TOMATO PASTE

This condensed puree is useful in sauces and soups because of its intense flavor.

CANNED TOMATOES

Can be used in a wide variety of dishes, from sauces and soups to stews and casseroles.

SUN-DRIED TOMATOES

These are very good in Italian recipes, particularly salads, pastas, and bread.

CANNED BEANS

You can buy a wide variety of canned beans, such as red kidney beans and chickpeas, which will save you time because you do not have to soak them or cook them. Cans of baked beans in tomato sauce are also indispensable for quick meals.

CANNED FISH

Canned fish, such as tuna, salmon, crab, anchovies, sardines, and pilchards, are versatile items to have in the pantry. They are particularly useful when added to pasta.

OLIVES

It is always useful to keep a can or bottle of olives on hand. They make ideal tapas for unexpected guests and are delicious in salads and pastas and on pizzas.

MUSTARDS

You can buy different types of mustard. Dijon mustard has a strong flavor and is used in dips and dressings. English mustard is very hot and useful in dips and dressings. American-style prepared mustard is milder, and goes well with a variety of savory dishes, especially meats.

PICKLED FOODS

Pickles, pickled onions, and capers make perfect accompaniments and garnishes for meat and vegetable dishes.

CHOCOLATE & UNSWEETENED COCOA

These are useful for desserts and baked goods, and also for some savory dishes.

VANILLA

You can buy vanilla in bean or liquid form (extract) as a flavoring. It is particularly delicious in desserts.

FISH & SEAFOOD	SPRING			SUMMER			FALL			WINTER		
	EARLY	MID	LATE	EARLY	MID	LATE	EARLY	MID	LATE	EARLY	MID	LATE
Clam (California)	●	●							●	●	●	●
Clam (East Coast/Pacific)	●	●	●	●	●	●	●	●	●	●	●	●
Cod	●	●	●	●	●	●	●	●	●	●	●	●
Crab, soft-shell		●	●	●	●	●	●					
Haddock				●	●	●	●	●				
Halibut	●	●	●	●	●	●	●	●				
Lobster	●	●	●	●	●	●	●			●		
Mussel (West Coast)	●								●	●	●	
Salmon (Atlantic)				●	●	●	●	●		●		
Salmon (Pacific)	●	●	●	●	●	●						
Sardines				●	●	●						
Scallop, bay (East Coast)							●		●			
Scallop, sea	●	●					●	●			●	●
Swordfish			●	●	●	●	●					
Tuna				●	●	●	●					
MEAT												
Beef	●	●	●	●	●	●	●	●	●	●	●	●
Lamb	●	●	●	●	●	●	●	●	●	●	●	●
Pork	●	●	●	●	●	●	●	●	●	●	●	●
POULTRY												
Chicken	●	●	●	●	●	●	●	●	●	●	●	●
Duck	●	●	●	●	●	●	●	●	●	●	●	●
Goose				●	●	●	●	●	●	●	●	●
Pheasant	●	●	●	●	●	●	●	●	●	●	●	●
Quail	●	●	●	●	●	●	●	●	●	●	●	●
Turkey	●	●	●	●	●	●	●	●	●	●	●	●
VEGETABLES												
Arugula	●	●	●									
Asparagus	●	●	●	●			●					●
Bean, green				●	●	●	●	●				
Bean, lima				●	●	●	●	●	●			
Bean, runner					●	●	●	●	●			
Beet	●					●	●	●		●	●	●
Broccoli	●	●	●				●	●				
Brussels sprouts (North)							●	●	●	●	●	●
Cabbage	●	●	●	●		●	●	●	●	●	●	●
Cabbage, Chinese							●	●				
Carrots				●		●	●					
Cauliflower	●	●	●				●	●	●	●	●	●
Celery				●	●	●	●			●	●	●
Chiles				●	●	●	●					
Cucumber			●	●	●	●						
Eggplant						●	●					
Fennel	●	●	●				●	●	●			
Garlic (fresh)			●	●	●	●	●	●				

Many fresh produce is now available year round. Because growing conditions vary from region to region, this is an approximate guide to peak seasons when vegetables, fruit, and herbs are at their best. The seasons for fish and shellfish apply to wild, not farmed, food.

	SPRING			SUMMER			FALL			WINTER		
	EARLY	MID	LATE	EARLY	MID	LATE	EARLY	MID	LATE	EARLY	MID	LATE
Globe artichoke	●	●	●									
Jerusalem artichoke	●						●	●		●	●	●
Leek	●						●	●		●	●	●
Lettuce	●	●	●				●	●	●	●	●	●
Mushroom (button)							●	●	●	●	●	●
Onion	●	●	●	●	●	●	●	●	●	●	●	●
Parsnip	●						●	●	●	●	●	●
Pea		●	●	●								
Pepper, sweet					●	●	●					
Potato	●	●	●	●	●	●	●	●	●	●	●	●
Pumpkin							●	●	●	●	●	●
Radish	●	●	●				●					
Rutabaga							●	●	●	●	●	●
Scallion	●	●	●	●	●	●						
Shallot	●	●	●									
Spinach	●	●	●				●	●	●			
Squash, winter (e.g. butternut)							●	●	●	●	●	●
Sweet corn			●	●	●	●	●					
Sweet potato										●	●	●
Tomato					●	●	●	●				
Turnip	●						●	●	●	●	●	●
Watercress	●	●	●	●	●	●	●	●	●	●	●	●
Zucchini and summer squash				●	●	●						
HERBS												
Basil			●	●	●	●	●					
Chives	●	●	●	●	●	●	●	●	●	●	●	●
Cilantro		●	●	●	●	●	●	●				
Dill			●	●	●	●	●					
Mint			●	●	●	●	●					
Oregano		●	●	●	●	●	●	●	●	●	●	●
Parsley, curly	●	●	●	●	●	●	●	●	●	●	●	●
Parsley, flat-leaf		●	●	●	●	●	●	●				
Rosemary	●	●	●	●	●	●	●	●	●	●	●	●
Sage	●	●	●	●	●	●	●	●	●	●	●	●
Tarragon				●	●	●	●	●				
Thyme	●	●	●	●	●	●	●	●	●	●	●	●
FRUIT												
Apple	●						●	●	●	●	●	●
Blackberry			●	●	●	●						
Blueberry				●	●	●						
Cherry			●	●	●	●						
Cranberry								●	●	●		
Grape						●	●	●				
Melon					●	●	●					
Orange and other citrus	●	●	●	●	●	●	●	●	●	●	●	●
Peach and nectarine			●	●	●	●	●					
Pear	●						●	●	●	●	●	●
Plum				●	●	●	●	●				
Raspberry				●	●	●	●	●	●			
Strawberry		●	●	●								

CONVERSION CHARTS

OVEN TEMPERATURES

FAHRENHEIT	CELSIUS	GAS MARK	OVEN HEAT
225°	110°	¼	very cool
250°	120°	½	very cool
275°	140°	1	cool
300°	150°	2	cool
325°	160°	3	moderate
350°	180°	4	moderate
375°	190°	5	moderately hot
400°	200°	6	moderately hot
425°	220°	7	hot
450°	230°	8	very hot
475°	240°	9	very hot

SPOON MEASUREMENTS

1 teaspoon of liquid = 5 ml

1 tablespoon of liquid = 15 ml

OTHER MEASUREMENTS

Liquid volume

US standard	Metric
1 fl oz/2 tbsp	30 ml
2 fl oz/¼ cup	60 ml
2¾ fl oz/⅓ cup	80 ml
4 fl oz/½ cup	120 ml
5 fl oz/⅔ cup	150 ml
6 fl oz/¾ cup	175 ml
8 fl oz/1 cup	240 ml
10 fl oz/1¼ cups	300 ml
12 fl oz/1½ cups	350 ml
16 fl oz/2 cups	475 ml
24 fl oz/3 cups	700 ml
4 cups/1 quart	950 ml
1.06 quarts	1 liter
4 quarts/1 gallon	3.8 liters

Weight

US standard	Metric
⅛ oz	5 g
¼ oz	10 g
1 oz	25 g
1¾ oz	50 g
2¾ oz	75 g
3 oz	85 g
3½ oz	100 g
5½ oz	150 g
8 oz	225 g
10½ oz	300 g
1 lb	450 g
1 lb 2 oz	500 g
2 lb 4 oz	1 kg
3 lb 5 oz	1.5 kg

Linear

US standard	Metric
1/16 inch	2 mm
⅛ inch	3 mm
¼ inch	5 mm
⅜ inch	8 mm
½ inch	1 cm
¾ inch	2 cm
1 inch	2.5 cm
2 inches	5 cm
3 inches	7.5 cm
4 inches	10 cm
8 inches	20 cm
12 inches/1 foot	30 cm
18 inches/1½ feet	46 cm
20 inches/1⅔ feet	50 cm

PREPARATION TECHNIQUES

You will find this section a valuable source of reference for all the basic preparation techniques you are likely to need in everyday cooking. There are also some advanced techniques for the more experienced cook.

GRIND

This term means to crush food, such as nuts or coffee beans, to a powder or into very small pieces. For this job, you can use a coffee grinder, food processor, or a mortar and pestle for a coarser result.

INFUSE

This technique involves steeping flavorful ingredients, such as herbs or spices, in a liquid in order to flavor it.

BARD

This means to wrap pieces of fat, such as bacon, around lean cuts of meat and poultry.

CRUSH

This technique is useful for bringing out the flavor of garlic and herbs.

BASTE

When you spoon juices or fat over food during cooking, this is known as "basting." It helps to keep the food moist and seal in the flavor.

FOLD

This involves mixing a light mixture into a heavier one using a spoon or spatula in a figure-eight movement. This is done to keep the air within the batter.

MARINATE

This term means to soak food in a marinade for a few hours or days to tenderize it and give it more flavor. You can marinate meat, poultry, fish, and vegetables.

BEAT

This technique involves using a fork, spoon, or electric mixer in a vigorous stirring motion to remove any lumps from sauces and incorporate air into omelets and cake batters.

DEGLAZE

After food has been cooked in a pan, a small amount of liquid, such as stock or wine, is stirred in to loosen browned sediments of food stuck to the bottom of the pan. This is called deglazing.

PUNCH DOWN

This entails punching the air out of bread dough after it has risen.

RUB IN

This is used mainly for pastry making. Using fingertips, the fat is rubbed into the flour, lifting it high over the bowl in order to trap air into the mixture.

RUB IN

CRUSH

GRIND

FOLD

SHRED

WHISK

CHIFFONADE

CLARIFY

You can clarify butter or a liquid. To clarify butter, heat it slowly to separate the milk solids, which sink to the bottom of the pan, skimming any foam off the top. To clarify a liquid, such as a stock, add egg whites and/or egg shells to it and simmer for 10 minutes, then cool and strain it. The egg whites or shells draw out the impurities.

SHRED

This technique involves using a small, sharp knife or grater to cut food into very thin lengths.

LINE

This means lining a pan with something to prevent food sticking to it during cooking. The most common method is to rub butter or oil over the surface of the pan, then cover with parchment paper before adding the food.

KNEAD

This technique uses the heel of the hand to pull and stretch bread dough in order to develop the gluten in the flour so that the bread will keep its shape when it has risen. You can also knead dough in a food processor or food mixer that has a dough hook attachment.

WHISK

Whisking involves beating a light mixture, such as cream and eggs, vigorously with a whisk to incorporate more air. You can use a balloon whisk (but it takes a lot of effort), an electric handheld mixer, a free-standing mixer, or a food processor with a whisk attachment.

SKIM

This term means to remove foam or fat from the surface of a simmering liquid with a large slotted spoon or a ladle.

ZEST

This means to remove the outer layer of a citrus fruit without the bitter pith.

CHIFFONADE

A French term meaning "made of rags," it refers to the effect you get when you roll leafy vegetables together, then slice them crossways with a sharp knife to make ribbons.

ENRICH

This means adding a rich ingredient to a dish in order to create a richer texture or flavor. For example, you could add butter to a dough, or cream to a sauce.

GLAZE

This involves brushing water, beaten egg, or sugar and water onto pastry before baking to give it a glossy shine (and make it crunchy if sugar is added).

EMULSIFY

Emulsification happens when one liquid is slowly added to another in a gradual stream while stirring or blending rapidly. For example, mayonnaise is made by adding oil in a slow stream to a beaten egg mixture while whisking or blending.

EMULSIFY

LARD

To lard means to insert strips of pork fat into a lean cut of meat to flavor it and keep it moist.

JULIENNE

This technique involves cutting food, such as carrots and celery, into fine batons or strips.

TENDERIZE

This involves pounding meat, such as a beef steak, with a mallet in order to break down the tough fibers. You can also tenderize meat by marinating it.

GREASE OR OIL

This is to rub a little butter or oil over the surface of a pan to prevent food from sticking to it during cooking.

STEEP

Steeping means to soak an ingredient in hot liquid in order to release its flavor into the liquid.

CUT

This method means to use a sharp knife to make an incision or separate a food into smaller pieces.

MASH

This means to reduce cooked food (usually potatoes or other root vegetables) to a pulp using a potato masher or ricer.

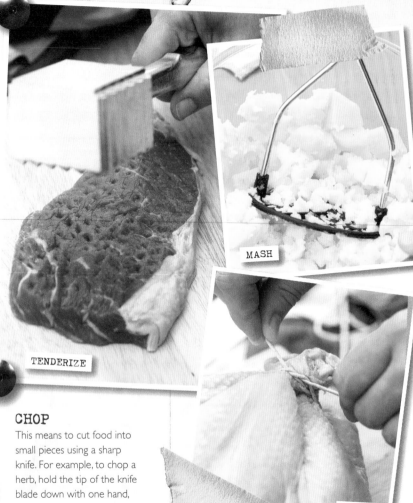

MASH

TENDERIZE

TRUSS

CHOP

This means to cut food into small pieces using a sharp knife. For example, to chop a herb, hold the tip of the knife blade down with one hand, then use your other hand to raise the handle of the knife up and down as you chop the herb. You can chop food coarsely or finely, depending on your requirements. Coarsely chopped means that the food will be left in larger pieces.

DRESS

This can mean to add a dressing to a salad, to decorate a dish before serving, or to pluck and truss poultry.

TRUSS

This means to pull a poultry or game bird into shape then secure with string or skewers before cooking. This technique is particularly useful for preventing stuffing from falling out of a bird.

CREAM

Creaming is similar to beating in that you use a fork, spoon, or electric mixer to beat ingredients together until they are smooth. This technique is usually associated with something rich and creamy, such as butter.

PUREE

This describes reducing food to a smooth pulp. You can do this by pushing food through a strainer or using a blender.

MACERATE

To macerate means to soak a food in a liquid, often alcohol, to soften it.

OPEN FREEZE

This technique means to freeze foods, uncovered, in a single layer. For example, you can cut fruit, such as mango, into small pieces, spread them out on a baking sheet, and freeze them uncovered. Then transfer the pieces individually to a freezer bag and use as required.

CRIMP

For this technique, use the finger and thumb of one hand and the index finger of the other hand to "pinch" pastry together around the edge of a pie or pasty. This gives it a decorative effect.

CURE

Curing means to preserve a food by salting or smoking it.

DEGORGE

This is soaking meat, poultry, or fish in cold water and salt to remove impurities. This term is also used for salting eggplants to remove their bitter juices.

DREDGE

This means to sprinkle flour onto a surface to roll out pastry, or to sprinkle confectioners' sugar or unsweetened cocoa over desserts.

SIFT

This technique involves shaking dry ingredients, such as flour, through a sifter to remove lumps and introduce more air into the mixture.

GRIND

This is to grind food, such as meat, into small pieces using a knife or grinder.

CROSSHATCH

To crosshatch means to score crisscross patterns on the surface of foods to let them absorb marinades or be removed from their skins. You can crosshatch the outer layer of fat on a cut of pork before cooking to let the fat drain and create a decorative effect.

GRATE

This means to shred food into small pieces. You can use a four-sided grater or food processor.

SHUCK

This term refers to removing the husks from corn and the shells from peas.

SNIP

This means using kitchen scissors to cut green leafy vegetables or herbs into very small pieces.

SIFT

CROSSHATCH

PUREE

EGGS & DAIRY

Nowadays we can buy a wide range of delicious eggs that are full of protein and are very easy to prepare and cook. Likewise, more dairy products are available than ever before and we can choose from an ever-increasing array of milk, yogurt, cream, butter, and cheese.

BUYING & STORING EGGS

Always buy your eggs from a reputable supplier, and do not buy any with cracked shells. Make sure the eggs are as fresh as possible by checking the expiration date on the carton. You can also check an egg's freshness by floating it in water: if it sinks to the bottom of the bowl horizontally, it is very fresh; if it stays vertical with its tip on the bottom, it is less fresh; if it floats to the top it is stale and should be discarded. Store your eggs, pointed ends down, in their carton at the back of a low shelf in the refrigerator. They should not be stored in the refrigerator door, where they will be subject to fluctuations in temperature each time the door is opened. Separated egg whites will keep in the refrigerator in a lidded container for up to 4 days, and in the freezer for up to 6 months. (You can freeze egg whites in ice-cube trays, then remove and store them in freezer-proof bags.)

Always label the container with the date of freezing and what it contains. Eggs are best cooked at room temperature, so remember to take them out of the refrigerator about an hour before they are needed, especially if you are planning to do some baking. Pasteurized liquid eggs are also available in cartons.

WHISKING EGG WHITES

Eggs that are 3–5 days old are best for whisking. Make sure that everything is clean and that your bowl is free of grease. Put the egg whites in a large bowl. If whisking by hand, use a large balloon whisk in an upward, circular movement. Alternatively, use a handheld electric mixer or free-standing food mixer. If the recipe calls for a "soft peaks" consistency, the mixture should form peaks that are soft and will flop over when the whisk or beaters are removed. If you need "firm peaks," the peaks should stand rigid.

KNOWING YOUR EGGS

COLL DUCK EGG

GOOSE EGG

QUAIL EGG

AYLESBURY DUCK EGG

FREE-RANGE HEN EGG

KHAKI CAMPBELL DUCK EGG

SCRAMBLING EGGS

Allow 2 eggs and 1 tablespoon of milk per person. Whisk together the eggs and milk in a bowl, then season with salt and pepper. Melt 1 tablespoon of butter in a nonstick pan, then pour in the egg mixture. Stir continuously over low heat for 5–7 minutes, until almost set, then remove from the heat. Stir for 1 more minute, then serve.

BOILING EGGS

To boil eggs, bring a small saucepan of water to a boil. Reduce the heat to a simmer, add a pinch of salt, then carefully add the eggs.

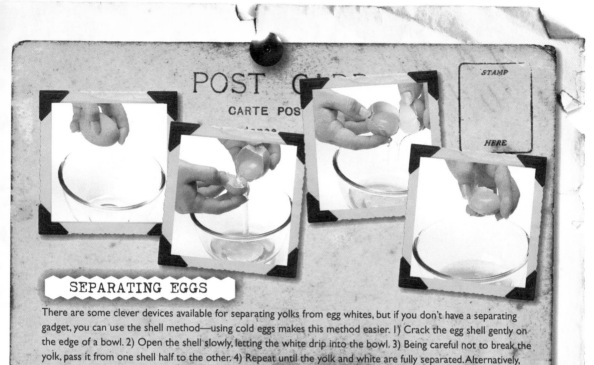

POST CARD

CARTE POSTALE

SEPARATING EGGS

There are some clever devices available for separating yolks from egg whites, but if you don't have a separating gadget, you can use the shell method—using cold eggs makes this method easier. 1) Crack the egg shell gently on the edge of a bowl. 2) Open the shell slowly, letting the white drip into the bowl. 3) Being careful not to break the yolk, pass it from one shell half to the other. 4) Repeat until the yolk and white are fully separated. Alternatively, open the egg into your hand, cradling the yolk gently, and let the white drip through your fingers to separate.

Simmer for 4–5 minutes for soft-boiled, and 9–10 minutes for hard-boiled (no longer, or a dark ring will appear around the yolk). Remove with a slotted spoon and plunge into cold water to prevent additional cooking.

FRYING EGGS

Heat 1 tablespoon of butter or oil in a skillet until hot (but not smoking). Break the eggs carefully into the skillet so that the yolks remain intact. Cook over medium heat for 3–4 minutes, until the white has set. Use a spatula to lift out the eggs for sunny-side up; alternatively, for easy-over, flip over and cook for another 1–2 minutes.

POACHING EGGS

Eggs need to be very fresh for poaching or they will break up in the water. You can use either a nonstick egg poacher or silicone poaching pods for this, or alternatively you can use the following method.

Fill a small skillet with enough water to cover an egg. Bring to a boil, then reduce the heat to a simmer. Break the egg carefully into a cup, then pour it gently into the boiling water so that the yolk does not break. Cook for 3–4 minutes; you can baste the egg with a little of the cooking liquid to ensure it is cooked. Lift it out with a slotted spoon and serve.

CODDLING EGGS

An egg coddler is a porcelain cup with a lid. Grease the coddler with butter, break an egg into it, season with salt and pepper, and loosely screw on the lid. Stand the coddler in a saucepan of boiling water, with the water up to the bottom of its lid, and simmer for 7–8 minutes. Remove and serve.

SAFETY

Eggs can carry harmful bacteria and may cause food poisoning if not thoroughly cooked, so do not give dishes with raw or lightly cooked eggs to people who may be particularly vulnerable, such as pregnant or breast-feeding women, babies and toddlers, the elderly, people who are ill, or convalescents.

KNOWING YOUR DAIRY

BUTTER

YOGURT

MILK

CHEDDAR

PARMESAN

CURD CHEESE

CLOTTED CREAM

STILTON

BUYING & STORING MILK

Milk is a good source of protein and calcium. The most commonly available is fresh cow's milk, which comes in whole (3½% fat), low-fat (the two types have less than 2% or 1% fat), and nonfat or skim (less than ½% fat). Most milk has been homogenized, which means that the fat has been spread throughout the milk so that there is no creamy layer on top. Buttermilk tastes a little like yogurt or thickened low-fat milk. Dry milk is a powdered form of milk with the moisture content removed; you can reconstitute it with water and use in place of fresh milk. Long-life milk has been heated quickly to about 300°F/149°C, then cooled and vacuum-packed to ensure a shelf-life without refrigeration of 6 months. You can also buy condensed milk, which is very thick and sweet, and evaporated milk, which is sterilized in cans. If you are sensitive to cow's milk, you can buy goat's milk or sheep's milk, or milk made from soybean or rice instead.

Most fresh milk has been pasteurized (heated then quickly cooled) in order to kill off any harmful bacteria, although some unpasteurized milk is available (see Safety box, below). Always check the expiration date on milk before you buy it, and store fresh milk, covered, in the refrigerator. Leaving milk out at room temperature for as little as 30 minutes is long enough to substantially effect its storage life.

BUYING & STORING YOGURT

Yogurt is made by fermenting milk with healthy bacteria. It has a slightly tangy taste and is a healthy choice because it is thick and creamy yet low in fat. Greek yogurt is the thickest and has the creamiest consistency. You can freeze yogurt for a healthy low-fat alternative to ice cream. Check the expiration date before buying, and store it in the refrigerator. Keep it covered when not in use.

BUYING & STORING BUTTER

Butter is made by churning cream until it separates into semisolids. It comprises at least 80% fat and the other 20% is made up of milk solids and water. Sometimes it is colored with annatto (a natural color made from the paste of seeds). Butter is available in salted and unsalted types: unsalted is essential for sweet dishes. You can also buy "spreadable" butter: this has been blended with oil so that it will stay soft and can be spread more easily. Make sure your butter

is always tightly wrapped to prevent it from absorbing odors. Check the expiration date on the packaging. Butter also freezes well, for up to 6 months in the freezer.

BUYING & STORING CREAM

Cream is made from the fattiest part of milk. It, therefore, has a higher fat content than milk, and a milder flavor. Half-and-half is a mixture of milk and cream and has the the lowest fat content (10–12%); it is ideal for sauces and soups. Light cream is preferred for pouring into drinks, such as coffee, but has a higher fat content (18–30% fat). Heavy cream, also known as heavy whipping cream, has a high fat content (36–40%) that is ideal for whipping and piping into decorative shapes. It is a delicious luxury for special occasions, perhaps to enrich a sauce or accompany a dessert. Sour cream (18–20% fat) has a slightly tangy taste and is ideal in savory dishes, as is the higher fat specialty crème fraîche (up to 50% fat). Other specialty creams include clotted cream (look for it at a specialty British food supplier), which is very thick. It is ideal on scones (sweet biscuits) or served with special desserts. All cream should be kept covered, stored in the refrigerator, and used by the expiration date on the carton. Heavy cream can be frozen up to 3 weeks.

BUYING & STORING CHEESE

Cheese is made from milk that is allowed to thicken and then separate into curds (semisolids) and whey (a liquid). Fresh cheeses are rindless and vary in consistency. Typical cheeses in this category are cream cheese and cottage cheese. Soft and semihard cheeses are firmer, and range from creamy soft cheeses with rinds, such as Brie, to firmer cheeses, such as Port Salut. Generally, the harder the cheese, the higher the fat content, and hard cheeses have the highest fat of all. They are often easy to grate, and range from cheddar cheese to Parmesan. Blue cheeses are also available: these have blue veins running through them and a strong flavor and aroma (the veins are made by a friendly bacteria). Blue cheese types include Gorgonzola and Stilton. You can also buy cheese made from goat's milk and sheep's milk.

Keep your cheese tightly wrapped. Store fresh cheese in the coldest part of the refrigerator, and the other cheeses in the warmest part. Hard cheeses can be grated ready for use and kept in the refrigerator for up to 1 week. Use cheeses by the expiration date. You can freeze hard cheeses, but they will have a crumblier texture when defrosted. Grated cheese also freezes well but is only suitable for cooking, not for adding to salads.

SAFETY
Unpasteurized milk is available from specialty suppliers, but there is still a risk of disease and, therefore, this milk should not be given to vulnerable people, especially pregnant or breast-feeding women, babies and toddlers, the elderly, people who are ill, or convalescents.

MEAT

Meat is rich in protein and easy to cook. It makes an excellent centerpiece to any meal, and you can choose from a wide range of roasts and cuts, from the economical to the indulgent, to suit any occasion.

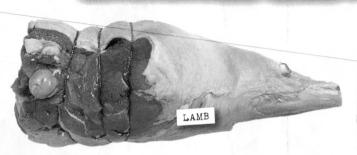

LAMB

BEEF

BUYING & STORING MEAT

Always buy your fresh meat from a reputable supplier. For lamb, choose firm, pinkish, marbled meat; avoid cuts that look dark and soggy. The fat should be cream-colored. For pork, choose moist, pinkish meat with white fat. Avoid any meat that looks oily or that has yellow fat. For beef, look for meat that is deep burgundy red; the fat should be cream-colored. Choose beef that has a marbling of fat through it—this will help to keep the meat moist during cooking. If you are buying meat to roast, plan about 6–12 oz/175–350 g per person, depending on whether the meat is on or off the bone. Once you get the meat home, unwrap it

and transfer it to a clean dish (the dish should have a lip deep enough to catch any juices). Cover with plastic wrap and store in the refrigerator away from any cooked meats. However, you can leave any prepackaged meat in its wrapping in the refrigerator and use by the expiration date. Unpackaged ground lamb, beef, and pork is best used within 1–2 days of purchase. Fresh cuts of beef and pork will keep in the refrigerator for 2–3 days, and cooked beef and pork can be refrigerated for 4–5 days. Fresh lamb cuts will keep for up to 4 days in the refrigerator. Before cooking, bring out the meat and let it reach room temperature for 30 minutes. You can freeze small cuts of beef or pork for

up to 6 months, and lamb for up to 3 months. Make sure you thaw the meat thoroughly in a refrigerator before cooking: allow 6 hours per 1 lb/450 g.

PREPARATION TECHNIQUES

There is a range of techniques you can use to prepare and/or improve your cuts of meat before cooking. Some of them are done purely for presentation, while other techniques help to tenderize the meat or facilitate thorough cooking.

LAMB CHOPS

Use a sharp knife to remove the excess fat around the edge.

PORK CHOPS & SIRLOIN STEAKS

Use a sharp knife to make incisions in the fat at intervals of 1 inch/2.5 cm around the edge. This helps prevent the meat from curling up at the sides during cooking.

CHUCK STEAK

Remove excess fat with a sharp knife. Slice across the grain and cut across the slices to form cubes.

PORK

TENDERIZE THIN CUTS OF MEAT

Put the meat between sheets of wax paper and pound with either a meat mallet or the bottom of a saucepan.

STUFF & TIE A BONELESS ROAST

Put it skin-side down and arrange the stuffing evenly over the surface. Roll up the meat from the thick end, tie a piece of clean string lengthwise around the meat, then knot it and trim off the ends. Tie additional pieces of string widthwise around the meat at intervals of 1 inch/2.5 cm. Knot each one in turn and trim the ends.

BUTTERFLY A LEG OF LAMB

Push a chef's knife into the cavity of the bone, then cut sideways to part the meat. Open it out and make a light incision down the center of the meat so that it stays open and flat.

PREPARE A RACK OF LAMB

Remove the skin and excess fat, leaving a layer of fat about ⅝ inch/15 mm thick. Cut off the bone at the back, then remove the fat from the ends of the bones (to a length of about 2 inches/5 cm). Use a knife to scrape out the meat from between the bones.

CHOOSING CUTS OF MEAT

There are many different cuts of meat available. Choosing the right cut will help to ensure the perfect result for your chosen recipe. When in doubt, ask your local butcher for advice.

BEEF

For roasting, choose tenderloin, rib-eye roast, or standing rib roast. T-bone, porterhouse, top loin, and sirloin are excellent steaks for broiling or grilling. For braising or stewing, use chuck, rump, or short rib.

PORK

For roasting, grilling, and frying, choose tender cuts from the loin and tenderloin that stand up to dry heat. Cuts from the shoulder and leg are tougher, and these are best cooked by slow, moist heat methods, such as braising and stewing. Chops, steaks, and cutlets are all terms referring to a slice of meat, but a steak may be thicker and a cutlet thinner. Medallions are boneless slices from the center loin.

VEAL

Much of the veal found in supermarkets is limited to roasts, chops, and scallops, but occasionally veal breast and ground veal are available, too. If availability is a problem, order ahead from a butcher.

LAMB

The leg is the most popular choice for roasting, but you can also roast the shoulder, rack of lamb, and loin. For broiling, try chops and steaks. Rib and loin chops are tender cuts; shoulder, arm, and blade chops from the arm and shoulder are noted by the lines of fat running through the meat. Finally, for stewing, braising, or casseroles, choose stew meat from the shoulder and neck for the best flavor.

COOKING & CARVING TECHNIQUES

Techniques for cooking and carving large pieces of meat are not difficult, but they do have to be performed properly in order to get the best out of the meat. Follow the instructions given here for perfect results every time.

ROASTING & CARVING A BONED ROAST

This technique is suitable for boned roasts of lamb, pork, and beef. Rub the surface with a little oil, followed by some salt and some crushed peppercorns (use a mortar and pestle for this). Place on a rack in a roasting pan, then roast in the oven, basting once or twice during cooking. Remove from the oven and cut off the strings. Wrap the meat in foil and let stand for 15–20 minutes. To carve, steady the meat with a fork, then carve slices downward from one end.

ROASTING & CARVING A LEG OF LAMB

Using a sharp knife, score a crisscross pattern in the fat, then rub all over the surface with a little oil, followed by some salt and freshly ground black pepper. Put the meat on a rack in a roasting pan and roast in the oven, basting once or twice during cooking. To test if the meat is cooked all the way through, pierce a skewer or knife into the thickest part. The juices that run out will be clear if the meat is cooked. If not, return it to the oven and cook until it is done. Remove from the oven and wrap the meat in foil. Let stand for 15–20 minutes. To carve, turn the leg meat-side up, then steady the meat with a fork. Start carving from the knuckle end. When you have finished, turn over the leg and carve horizontal slices.

USING A MEAT THERMOMETER

A meat thermometer is a useful device for testing whether a roast of meat is cooked thoroughly. Thorough cooking is particularly important in the case of pork, which can carry harmful bacteria and cause food poisoning if not cooked all the way through. Simply insert the thermometer into the thickest part of the meat at the start of cooking. Be careful to make sure that the thermometer does not come into contact with any bone, because this could produce a false reading. When the thermometer reaches the required temperature, the meat is cooked. The recommended temperatures for different meats are shown on the next page.

OVEN TEMPERATURES & ROASTING TIMES

Please note that individual oven temperatures and cooking times vary, so the following cooking times are only an approximate guide. Remember to preheat the oven before cooking in order to get the best results.

MEAT	JOINT	WEIGHT	TEMPERATURE	COOKING TIME
LAMB	Whole leg	5 lb 8 oz/2.5 kg	350°F/180°C	2¼ hours (medium rare)
				or 2½ hours (well done)
LAMB	Whole shoulder	5 lb 8 oz/2.5 kg	350°F/180°C	2¼ hours (medium rare)
				or 2½ hours (well done)
PORK	Loin (boned)	5 lb 8 oz/2.5 kg	350°F/180°C	3 hours at lower temperature, then
			425°F/220°C	20 minutes at higher temperature (well done)
PORK	Shoulder (boned)	5 lb 8 oz/2.5 kg	350°F/180°C	3 hours at lower temperature, then
			425°F/220°C	20 minutes at higher temperature (well done)
BEEF	Sirloin	5 lb 8 oz/2.5 kg	400°F/200°C	1¾ hours (rare), 2¼ hours (medium rare),
				or 2½ hours (well done)
BEEF	3-rib prime roast	5 lb/2.25 kg	450°F/230°C	15 minutes at the higher temperature, then
			350°F/180°C	1 hour at the lower temperature (rare)

OVEN TEMPERATURES & HEAT DESCRIPTIONS

You may come across recipes that do not give a specific temperature: instead they will simply recommend cooking in a "moderate" or "hot" oven. Here is a list of these heat descriptions and their correct temperatures.

OVEN HEAT DESCRIPTION	FAHRENHEIT	CELSIUS
VERY COOL	225–250°	110–120°
COOL	275–300°	140–150°
MODERATE	325–350°	160–180°
MODERATELY HOT	375–400°	190–200°
HOT	425°	220°
VERY HOT	450–475°	230–240°

POULTRY & GAME

Poultry is rich in protein, and quick and easy to prepare and cook. Some birds, such as chicken and turkey, can be a low-fat choice as long as the fatty skin is removed, and they are very versatile. Duck is fattier, but makes a good dinner-party choice.

BUYING & STORING POULTRY AND GAME

Always buy your poultry and game as fresh as possible and from a reputable supplier. Choose plump birds that have unblemished skin, and make sure that any wrapping or packaging is intact.

As soon as you get it home, remove the packaging (if it is a fresh bird) and transfer the giblets (if any) to a separate bowl. Place the bird on a rack in a dish, then cover it and any giblets loosely with plastic wrap and store in the refrigerator. Keep it well away from cooked meats to prevent any cross-contamination. Whole birds will keep for 1–2 days in the refrigerator, and giblets no longer than 1 day. Frozen birds can be stored in the freezer in their original packaging. Thaw in the refrigerator thoroughly before cooking; you will need to allow 5 hours per 1 lb/450 g for a chicken and 6 hours per 1 lb/450 g for a turkey. Game birds are available fresh when in season and frozen all year round. If they are truly wild birds and not farmed, they will have a lower fat content and should, therefore, be wrapped in bacon or pork fat during roasting. Older birds are not recommended for roasting—they are more suited to soups, casseroles, and stews. Game animals, such as venison and rabbit, tend to be less tender than farmed animals because they get more exercise in the wild. They should, therefore, be cooked slowly until tender, but not overcooked. Braising is a good method for keeping the meat moist, or it can be roasted if wrapped first in bacon or pork fat.

TYPES OF BIRD

In addition to the flavor, the choice of bird may depend on the occasion and how many people you are catering for.

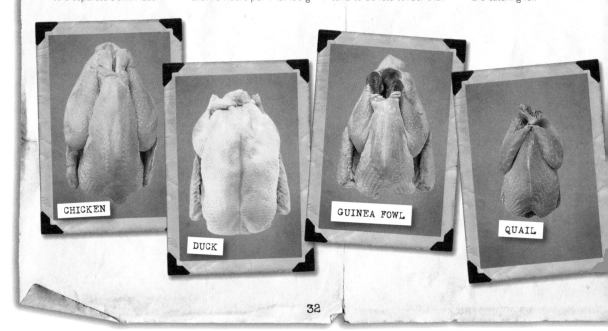

CHICKEN

DUCK

GUINEA FOWL

QUAIL

CHICKEN

There are many different varieties of chicken available. You can buy whole birds already prepared for the oven or frozen. You can also buy a variety of cuts—wing, breast, leg, thigh, or drumstick—or you can cut up a whole bird yourself. Chicken is delicious roasted, steamed, poached, broiled, casseroled, grilled, chargrilled, stir-fried, pan-fried, or deep-fried. A Rock Cornish hen is a small chicken, at 2½ lb/1.1 kg, suitable for a single serving. Broiler-fryers are young birds that typically weigh 3½ lb/1.6 kg and are best for frying and broiling; they have the best flavor. Roasters weigh 2½–5 lb/1.1–2.25 kg and are best for roasting.

POUSSIN

A French term, poussin is a young, small chicken weighing up to 1 lb/450 g.

GUINEA FOWL

This bird is related to the chicken and the partridge, and has light and dark meat and a strong flavor. Since guinea fowl has a low fat content, it is most suited to moist cooking methods such as casseroling. You can wrap it in bacon rashers or pork fat and roast it.

TURKEY

These birds are much larger than chickens—some can grow to a massive 70 lb/ 31.5 kg—but the trend is now for much smaller birds. This is because turkey suppliers would like to encourage their use all year round, instead of just during Thanksgiving and other holiday periods. Turkeys have similar uses to chickens, and you can often interchange them with chickens in recipes. You can buy whole birds already prepared for the oven or frozen. You can also buy separate cuts, such as breast joints or drumsticks. Turkey is particularly suitable for roasting, casseroling, braising, stir-frying, or pan-frying.

DUCK

Ducks are available whole, fresh, and frozen. Breast and leg cuts are also available. Duck is fattier than chicken or turkey, and is suitable for roasting, grilling, or pan-frying. Duck is often served with a tart fruit sauce.

PARTRIDGE

This game bird has dark flesh and an earthy flavor. Its flesh can be tough so is best braised, stewed, or casseroled. It can also be roasted.

GOOSE

Geese are larger than ducks, and can be bought fresh, although they are more often bought frozen. Although they

are popular during holidays and at Christmas time, especially in Europe, they have become less popular year-round because of their very high fat content. Geese are best roasted, pot-roasted, braised, or stewed. It is also a good idea to serve them accompanied with a tart fruit sauce in order to cut through any fatty aftertaste.

PHEASANT

These are medium-size game birds. The male has more brilliant plumage than the female, however, the female is juicier and more tender. Young pheasants can be roasted, but older birds should be wrapped in bacon or pork fat during roasting; they can also be braised, casseroled, or stewed.

QUAIL

These small game birds are related to the partridge. The American variety has lean but lighter flesh, whereas the European variety has lean, medium-dark flesh. Both types have a sweet flavor. Quails are suitable for roasting, pot-roasting, braising, barbecuing, casseroling, or broiling. Their small eggs have a speckled brown shell and a rich flavor.

VENISON

Deer is a popular game animal and the meat is available wild or farmed. It is low in cholesterol, and usually available as leg or saddle cuts, or as steaks. The best meat comes from a male deer under the age of two years. Venison meat is dry and more suited to casseroles.

PREPARATION & COOKING TECHNIQUES

It is essential to cook poultry all the way through in order to kill off any potentially harmful bacteria. If a bird is not cooked through when tested, return it to the oven to finish cooking, even if you have to exceed the recommended cooking time.

MAKING CHICKEN STOCK

Chicken stock is easy to prepare and is ideal for adding to soups and sauces. It can be stored, covered with plastic wrap, in the refrigerator for 2–3 days. You can also freeze it for up to 6 months. Put the chicken carcass into a large saucepan with 1 chopped onion, 1 sliced carrot, 1 chopped celery stalk, and 1 chopped leek. Add 1 bay leaf and 1 sprig of thyme, 3 stalks of parsley, and some cracked black peppercorns. Cover with water and bring to a boil, then use a slotted spoon to skim off any foam from the surface. Reduce the heat, cover, and let simmer for 2–3 hours. Strain into a large bowl and discard the solids. Use the stock as required.

ROASTING A LARGE CHICKEN OR A TURKEY

First wipe the bird inside and out with paper towels. If you are going to stuff it, pull back the skin around the neck cavity and insert the stuffing into the neck end only (do not overfill the bird or it will not cook through properly). If you are not stuffing the bird, simply season the cavity. Pull the skin over the top, then pull up the wings and tie with string. Pull the legs together and tie with string. Rub butter or oil over the skin of the bird, then season to taste with salt and pepper. Transfer to a wire rack in a roasting pan, and roast in a preheated oven, basting occasionally, until cooked through and tender. To test, insert a sharp knife or skewer into the thickest part of the bird; if the juices run clear, the bird is cooked. If not, return it to the oven and cook until done. Remove from the oven and let rest, covered in foil, for 15–20 minutes before carving.

ROASTING A GOOSE

Wipe the goose inside and out with paper towels and pull out any excess fat from inside. Season well with salt and pepper. If you are going to stuff the goose, insert the stuffing as far as possible in the neck flap end, securing the flap with a skewer. Prick the goose all over with a fork, lay on a rack in a roasting pan, and place in a preheated oven. To test that it is cooked all the way through, insert a skewer into the thickest part of the bird; if the juices run clear, the bird is cooked. Remove from the oven and let rest for 20 minutes before carving.

OVEN TEMPERATURES & ROASTING TIMES

Individual oven temperatures and cooking times vary, so cooking times are approximate. Preheat the oven before cooking.

BIRD	WEIGHT	TEMPERATURE	COOKING TIME
CHICKEN	6 lb 8 oz/3 kg	400°F/200°C	2¼ hours
TURKEY	11 lb/5 kg	350°F/180°C	3½ hours
	18 lb/8 kg	350°F/180°C	4¾–5 hours
QUAIL	1 lb/450 g	400°F/200°C	30 minutes
GOOSE	11 lb/5 kg	425°F/ 220°C	30 minutes at higher temperature,
		350°F/180°C	then for 2–3 hours at lower temperature
DUCK	5 lb 8 oz/2.5 kg	425°F/ 220°C	20 minutes at higher temperature,
		350°F/180°C	then for 2 hours at lower temperature

CARVING A LARGE BIRD

Place the cooked bird breast-side up on a clean cutting board. Use a carving knife to cut between one wing and the side of the breast. Remove the wing and cut thin, downward slices through the breast meat. Repeat with the other side, reserving the wings and the breast slices. Pull out one leg and cut through the bone. Repeat with the other side. Slice the meat from the thighs and drumsticks. Serve the wings and the meat slices.

ROASTING & CARVING A DUCK

Wipe the duck inside and out with paper towels. Duck has a high fat content, so remove any surplus fat. Season inside the tail cavity and insert a bay leaf. Transfer the bird to a wire rack in a roasting pan. Use a fork to prick holes all over it, then season with salt and pepper. Roast in a preheated oven until cooked through and tender (turn and baste it halfway through the cooking time). To test that the bird is cooked all the way through, insert a sharp knife or skewer into the thickest part of the bird; if the juices run clear, the bird is cooked. To serve the duck, divide it by cutting it in half lengthwise. Alternatively, use a sharp knife to separate the legs from the body, then cut off the wings. Remove the breast meat and slice it. Serve the legs, wings, and slices of breast meat.

CUTTING UP A WHOLE BIRD

1 To cut a large raw bird into pieces, remove any string and place it on a clean cutting board, breast-side up, with the legs pointing toward you.

2 Using a sharp knife, cut the skin between one leg and the side of the breast, then use your hand to press the leg down flat to the board. Do the same with the other leg. Cut through the bone attaching one of the legs and remove the leg from the body. Do the same for the other side.

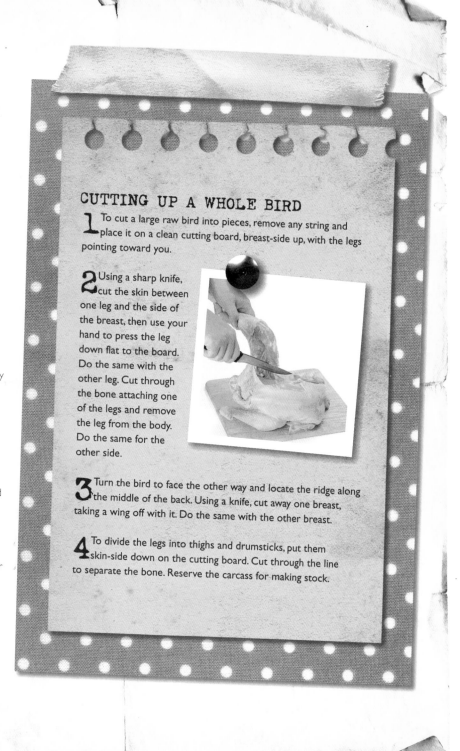

3 Turn the bird to face the other way and locate the ridge along the middle of the back. Using a knife, cut away one breast, taking a wing off with it. Do the same with the other breast.

4 To divide the legs into thighs and drumsticks, put them skin-side down on the cutting board. Cut through the line to separate the bone. Reserve the carcass for making stock.

HERBS & SPICES

There is a wide range of fresh herbs available all year round in your local supermarket, as well as a tempting array of fragrant and exotic spices. You can also buy frozen herbs, which are a good substitute when fresh herbs are unavailable. It is a good idea to keep some flowerpots of fresh herbs on a windowsill and a selection of dried herbs and spices in your pantry.

BUYING & STORING HERBS & SPICES

If you buy fresh herbs as plants, place them on a windowsill, where they can get plenty of light, and water them regularly. Basil, in particular, needs plenty of water, so make sure you do not let it dry out. Packaged fresh herbs should be stored in their wrapping in the refrigerator. If you grow herbs in your garden, after picking keep them in a jar of clean water until you are ready to use them. Store dried herbs and ground spices in a cool, dark place, such as an airy cupboard. Use all fresh herbs by their expiration date, and go through your pantry regularly and throw out any dried herbs and spices that are past their best.

TARRAGON

The dark green pointed leaves of tarragon have an aromatic, aniseed-like flavor. It adds a distinctive flavor to poultry, fish, eggs, sauces, salads, and dressings. It is best to use this herb on its own, because its strong flavor can overpower other herbs if mixed with them.

BASIL

There are many species of this herb. It thrives in a warm, Mediterranean climate, so in cold climates it will do better indoors on a windowsill with plenty of sunshine and water. It has a sweet, aromatic flavor, and is particularly good with tomatoes and mozzarella cheese. It is also delicious with poultry, fish and seafood, salads, and sauces. This herb is fragile and should, therefore, be added to recipes toward the end of the cooking time.

THYME

This herb comes in different varieties, and several of them are commonly used in cooking. The leaves add a pungent, aromatic flavor to meat, poultry, egg, and potato dishes, and are good in soups, sauces, roasts, casseroles, and stews.

OREGANO

This green herb is related to marjoram. It has a pungent flavor and should be used sparingly. It is popular in Italian cooking, particularly on pizzas, and adds an aromatic flavor to meat, poultry, eggs, and cheese.

CILANTRO

This pungent herb has bright green leaves and is very popular in Mediterranean and Asian cooking. It adds a distinctive flavor to salads, cooked vegetables, and stir-fries.

FENNEL

There are two types of fennel. One has a bulbous base, which can be cooked and used like a vegetable; the other variety has no bulb. Fennel has a strong aniseed flavor. The leaves of both types can be snipped into soups and sauces, and are excellent with fish and egg dishes.

MARJORAM

This ancient herb has pale green leaves and a delicate, sweet flavor. It is ideal with meat, poultry, cheese, tomatoes, eggs, dressings, and stir-fries.

ROSEMARY

The silvery, needle-shaped leaves of rosemary have a strong aromatic flavor. It is used in soups, salads, roasts, stuffings, dressings, and marinades, as well as on pizzas. The herb also makes delicious skewers for kebabs. It pairs particularly well with potatoes and bread, as well as meat, poultry, fish, and eggs.

BAY

The leaves of this aromatic herb come from the Mediterranean laurel tree. The fresh leaves, if you can get them, have more flavor than the dried, but either type will add a good, pungent flavor to soups, sauces, stocks, and casseroles. They are usually discarded once the food has absorbed their flavor.

SAGE

This herb has grayish oval leaves and a pungent, slightly bitter taste. It is very common in stuffings, especially those containing onion, and is excellent with pork, poultry, beans, cheese, rice, and pasta.

CHERVIL

The dark green, curly leaves of chervil have an aromatic flavor with a hint of aniseed. It is especially good in chicken, fish, and egg dishes.

MINT

There are many species of mint, the two best-known being peppermint and spearmint. Peppermint has a more peppery flavor, while spearmint has a fresher mint taste. Mint is a hardy plant and can take over a herb garden if not carefully controlled. Use it to flavor cooked potatoes, peas, sauces, soups, meat dishes, desserts, and drinks.

DILL

This herb has feathery green leaves and a mild flavor. Dill is excellent with fish, as well as in salads, cheese dishes, and sauces.

CHIVES

These relatives of the onion family have long, hollow stems and edible purple flowers. The fresh stems are snipped into small pieces and added to salads, soups, cream cheese, and egg dishes. You can also buy them frozen and dried.

PARSLEY

This versatile herb is rich in vitamins A and C and comes in many varieties. The two most popular types have green leaves that are either curly or flat. Curly parsley is common all year round, while flat-leaf Italian parsley may be found only in some supermarkets and specialty delicatessens. Parsley is used in a wide range of dishes, including soups, salads, sauces, stir-fries, and casseroles, as well as stuffings, dressings, and marinades. It adds a spicy, lingering flavor to meat, poultry, fish, eggs, and vegetables, and helps to offset the sulfur aftertaste of garlic. It also makes an attractive garnish, particularly the flat-leaf variety.

TYPES & USES OF SPICES

Spices used to be costly when international travel was comparatively slow and difficult, but now they are less expensive and more widely available.

PAPRIKA

This spice is made from ground red bell pepper pods and its flavor can vary from mild, sweet, and pungent to fiery hot. It is excellent in salads and as a garnish. It also goes well with meat, poultry, eggs, vegetables, cream cheese, pasta, rice, and beans.

CARDAMOM

This aromatic spice is related to ginger and has a pungent lemon flavor. You can grind and use the whole pod, or use just the seeds inside. Cardamom is widely used in Asian and Middle Eastern dishes, and adds a distinctive flavor to soups, stews, curries, pastry, bread, and cakes.

ALLSPICE

This small berry comes from the West Indies and South America and has a sweet flavor of nutmeg, cinnamon, and cloves. You can buy it whole or ground. It is used with meat, onions, and fruit desserts, as well as in cakes and bread.

MUSTARD

This hot, acrid spice is available as whole seeds, ground, or processed into a paste that ranges in intensity from mild to strong. It goes well with meat, poultry, seafood, eggs, beans, potatoes, bread, cheese, cream and butter sauces, marinades, relishes, and condiments.

CHILI POWDER

This powdered mixture of spices includes dried chiles, cumin, coriander, and cloves. It has a fiery heat but you can also buy mild chili powder. Use it to flavor soups and stews. It goes well with seafood, meat, poultry, vegetables, beans, and eggs.

FENNEL SEEDS

You can buy fennel seeds whole or ground. They have a sweet, mildly aniseed flavor and can be used in savory and sweet dishes, including marinades, pizzas, stuffings, bread, cakes, cookies, and a variety of desserts and drinks.

STAR ANISE

This star-shaped brown pod comes from an Asian tree. It has a warm, aromatic, slightly bitter aniseed flavor and is available whole or ground. It is popular in Chinese cooking, and is used in marinades, stir-fries, casseroles, cakes, fruit, and some drinks. It goes particularly well with pork, poultry, and fish.

CARAWAY

These seeds have a nutty, aniseed flavor and can be bought whole or ground. They are popular in German and Austrian cookery.

JUNIPER

These berries are available dried and are usually crushed to release their pungent pine flavor. Use them to flavor various meats.

CAYENNE PEPPER

This type of pepper is made from tropical chiles and it has a hot, spicy flavor. Use it to add a kick to South American and Caribbean dishes. It is especially good with seafood and condiments.

PEPPERCORNS

The dried berries from the pepper plant come in black, white, and green. Black peppercorns are the most widely used, and are available whole, cracked, or ground. They deteriorate quickly when ground, so it is best to buy them whole and grind them yourself. They have an aromatic flavor and can be used in almost every savory recipe and some sweet fruit dishes, such as balsamic strawberries.

CINNAMON

This spice comes from the bark of a tropical tree. The bark is dried and curled into quills or sticks; it can also be bought ground. Cinnamon has a sweet, aromatic smell and flavor, and is popular in Middle Eastern dishes. It is used to flavor a wide range of savory and sweet dishes, such as stews, curries, pies, bread, and cakes, and a whole host of desserts and drinks.

NUTMEG

Nutmeg has a sweet, fragrant flavor and is available whole or ground. It is used in a wide variety of savory and sweet dishes, from meat, poultry, vegetables, beans, rice, cheese, and eggs to chocolate, fruit, cream sauces, and drinks.

CORIANDER

The dried seeds of the coriander plant are fragrant and lemony and can be used whole or ground. They are popular in marinades, condiments, curries, and casseroles, and go particularly well with meat, poultry, fish, cheese, vegetables, beans, chocolate, and jelly.

CLOVES

These come from the buds of the tropical clove tree. The dried brown buds are sold whole or powdered, and have a sweet, pungent flavor. Push whole cloves into ham, pork, onions, and oranges to flavor them, or use them ground in soups, stews, bread, cakes, desserts, and condiments. You can also use them whole in drinks such as mulled wine (but always remove whole cloves before serving).

APPLE PIE SPICE

This blend of spices usually consists of cinnamon, nutmeg, and cardamom. It has a warm, sweet flavor and is delicious in fruit desserts, bread, cakes, cookies, pies, and drinks.

CUMIN

These dried seeds have a pungent, nutty flavor and are also available ground. Cumin is popular in Asian and Mexican cooking, and goes well with beef, pork, salmon, shellfish, beans, pasta, eggs, cheese, and rice.

FIVE SPICE

Chinese five-spice seasoning is, as its name implies, a blend of five spices, usually cloves, cinnamon, fennel seeds, Sichuan peppercorns, and star anise. It has a sweet, pungent flavor and is popular in Chinese and Vietnamese cooking. It is especially good in stir-fries.

CURRY POWDER

This powder contains a mixture of spices, including cardamom, chiles, cloves, coriander, fenugreek, and turmeric. It is available mild or hot, and is used in curries, cream sauces, and condiments. It also goes well with beef, chicken, turkey, seafood, root vegetables, rice, eggs, and cheese.

TURMERIC

This spice comes from the root of a tropical plant and has a pungent, somewhat bitter flavor. The powdered variety has a bright orange-yellow color, so is used to tint foods as well as to flavor them.

GINGER

Ginger is available fresh or dried. The fresh root has a warm, lemon flavor and can be used chopped or grated. It is especially useful in marinades, salads, soups, stews, and stir-fries; it can also be preserved in syrup. Powdered ginger has a more pungent, spicy flavor and is particularly good with fruit, cookies, and condiments.

BAKING

There is nothing like the aroma of freshly-baked bread, pastry, cakes, and cookies to stimulate the appetite. Baking these items for yourself is very satisfying, and the mouthwatering aromas will prove to be an irresistible temptation for friends and family.

MAKING BREAD AT HOME

Making your own bread does not have to be difficult—anyone can make delicious loaves and rolls with the minimum of effort. The key to making perfect bread is to use the right ingredients at the right temperature. Always use bread flour instead of ordinary flour: bread flour has a higher gluten content than ordinary flour, which increases the elasticity of the dough. You can use any of the different kinds of yeast, but each has a different method for breadmaking. You also need to use the correct quantities. One envelope of dry yeast is the same as scant 1 tbsp dry yeast or 1 cake compressed fresh yeast. When you add water, make sure it is lukewarm because, if it is too hot, it will kill the yeast.

KEY TECHNIQUES FOR MAKING DOUGH

Making the perfect dough can be straightforward, but it is important to follow a certain procedure to achieve good results every time.

PUNCHING DOWN

After letting the dough rise for the first time for about an hour, simply punch your fist into the risen dough so that it collapses and releases the air. Then turn the dough out onto a floured work surface (some of it may need scraping out) and knead it for about 1 minute, until it has lost its cold feel and has an even temperature.

RISING

This stage literally means that the yeast is still active. To do this, after punching down the dough, divide and shape it as required. Cover and let it rise for a second (but shorter) time, until the dough has doubled in size.

FRESH YEAST

Crush this in a pitcher with a little warm water, then cover and let stand until the surface starts to bubble.

DRY YEAST

Sprinkle the active dry yeast over a little warm water in a pitcher, then stir in a pinch of sugar. Cover and let stand until it froths.

INSTANT OR QUICK YEAST

Mix this yeast straight into the flour before the warm water is added.

FLOUR

Keep flour fresh by storing it in an airtight container in a cool, dry place. White flours will keep for 6-8 months, whole wheat flours, for up to 2 months.

CORNSTARCH

This powdery flour is made from corn kernels and is used for thickening sauces, soups, and desserts. It is usually mixed with a small quantity of cold liquid to make a smooth paste before being added to hot dishes.

ALL-PURPOSE WHITE FLOUR

This flour is used for thickening sauces as well as for making batters and pastry.

SELF-RISING FLOUR

All-purpose flour that has had baking powder and salt added is known as self-rising flour. It is used for making cakes and cookies.

BREAD FLOUR

This flour is used for making bread. It contains a high level of gluten, which helps to give the bread dough its elasticity. If you are using a whole wheat type, keep it in an airtight container in the refrigerator.

WHOLE WHEAT FLOUR

This flour has a stronger flavor than white flour and contains wheat germ, which means it has a higher fiber, fat, and nutrient content. Store in an airtight container in the refrigerator.

RYE FLOUR

A heavy, dark flour, rye flour has less gluten than all-purpose flour and whole wheat flour.

BAKING & STORING BREAD

The dough will keep, covered, in the refrigerator for up to a day before baking. To bake the bread, you will need a hot oven, so make sure you preheat it beforehand. Underbaked bread has a moist, doughlike consistency and flavor, so it is always better to overbake if necessary. To test if the bread is properly baked, remove it from the oven, turn it out of its pan, and use your knuckles to give it a sharp tap on the bottom. If it sounds hollow, the bread is done. If it does not, return it to the oven and bake for another 5 minutes, or until the bread is properly baked. When it is done, remove from the oven and let cool on a wire rack. If you want a soft crust, cover the loaf with a clean dish towel while it is cooling. Freshly baked bread will keep, covered, for 2–3 days at room temperature, but no longer because it has no added preservatives. You can also keep it wrapped in the refrigerator for up to a week, or wrap it in a freezer bag and freeze it for up to a month.

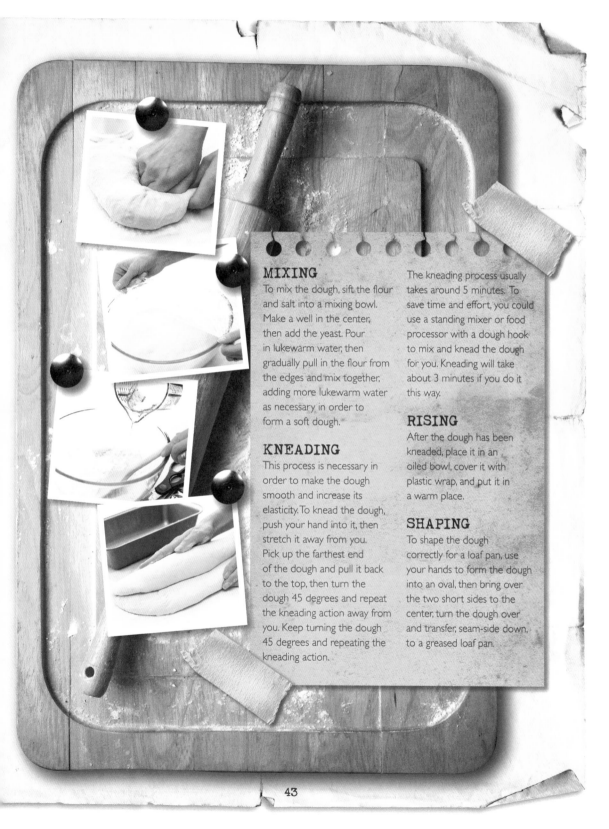

MIXING

To mix the dough, sift the flour and salt into a mixing bowl. Make a well in the center, then add the yeast. Pour in lukewarm water, then gradually pull in the flour from the edges and mix together, adding more lukewarm water as necessary in order to form a soft dough.

KNEADING

This process is necessary in order to make the dough smooth and increase its elasticity. To knead the dough, push your hand into it, then stretch it away from you. Pick up the farthest end of the dough and pull it back to the top, then turn the dough 45 degrees and repeat the kneading action away from you. Keep turning the dough 45 degrees and repeating the kneading action.

The kneading process usually takes around 5 minutes. To save time and effort, you could use a standing mixer or food processor with a dough hook to mix and knead the dough for you. Kneading will take about 3 minutes if you do it this way.

RISING

After the dough has been kneaded, place it in an oiled bowl, cover it with plastic wrap, and put it in a warm place.

SHAPING

To shape the dough correctly for a loaf pan, use your hands to form the dough into an oval, then bring over the two short sides to the center, turn the dough over and transfer, seam-side down, to a greased loaf pan.

CLASSIC
RECIPES

Chicken Noodle Soup

SERVES 4–6
INGREDIENTS

- 2 skinless chicken breasts
- 5 cups water or
  chicken stock
- 3 carrots, peeled and cut
  into ½-inch/1-cm slices
- 3 oz/85 g vermicelli
  (or other small noodles)
- salt and pepper
- fresh tarragon leaves,
  to garnish

1 Place the chicken breasts in a large saucepan, add the water, and bring to a simmer. Cook for 25–30 minutes. Skim any foam from the surface, if necessary. Remove the chicken from the pan and keep warm.

2 Continue to simmer the liquid, add the carrots and vermicelli, and cook for 4–5 minutes.

3 Thinly slice or shred the chicken breasts and place in warmed soup bowls.

4 Season the soup with salt and pepper to taste and pour over the chicken. Serve garnished with the tarragon.

COOK'S TIP
Clean hands are the best tools for shredding cooked chicken, flaking cooked fish, crumbling cheese, and tearing delicate salad greens and herbs.

Split Pea & Ham Soup

SERVES 6–8

INGREDIENTS

- 2½ cups split green peas
- 1 tbsp olive oil
- 1 large onion,
  finely chopped
- 1 large carrot,
  finely chopped
- 1 celery stalk,
  finely chopped
- 4 cups chicken stock or
  vegetable stock
- 4 cups water
- 8 oz/225 g lean smoked
  ham, finely diced
- ¼ tsp dried thyme
- ¼ tsp dried marjoram
- 1 bay leaf
- salt and pepper

1 Rinse the peas under cold running water. Put in a saucepan and cover generously with water. Bring to a boil and boil for 3 minutes, skimming off the foam from the surface. Drain the peas.

2 Heat the oil in a large saucepan over medium heat. Add the onion and cook for 3–4 minutes, stirring occasionally, until just softened. Add the carrot and celery and cook for 2 minutes.

3 Add the peas, pour over the stock and water, and stir to combine. Bring just to a boil and stir the ham into the soup. Add the thyme, marjoram, and bay leaf. Reduce the heat, cover, and cook gently for 1–1½ hours, until the ingredients are very soft. Remove and discard the bay leaf.

4 Taste and adjust the seasoning, then ladle into warmed soup bowls and serve.

Hints & Tips

Recipe: _____
Serves: _____
Ingredients: _____
_____
_____
_____
_____
_____

Method: _____
_____
_____
_____
_____
_____
_____
_____
_____
_____

Recipe: _____
Serves: _____
Ingredients: _____
_____
_____
_____
_____
_____

Method: _____
_____
_____
_____
_____
_____
_____
_____
_____
_____

Just a Note...

_____
_____
_____
_____
_____
_____

Just a Note...

_____
_____
_____
_____
_____
_____

Hints & Tips

_____

_____

_____

_____

_____

_____

_____

_____

_____

_____

_____

_____

_____

_____

_____

Recipe: _____

Serves: _____

Ingredients: _____
_____
_____
_____
_____

Method: _____
_____
_____
_____
_____
_____
_____
_____
_____

Recipe: _____

Serves: _____

Ingredients: _____
_____
_____
_____
_____

Method: _____
_____
_____
_____
_____
_____
_____
_____
_____

Just a Note...

_____

_____

_____

_____

_____

_____

_____

Just a Note...

_____

_____

_____

_____

_____

_____

_____

Hints & Tips

Recipe: _____
Serves: _____
Ingredients: _____
_____
_____
_____
_____

Method: _____
_____
_____
_____
_____
_____
_____
_____
_____
_____
_____

Recipe: _____
Serves: _____
Ingredients: _____
_____
_____
_____
_____

Method: _____
_____
_____
_____
_____
_____
_____
_____
_____
_____
_____

Just a Note...
_____
_____
_____
_____
_____
_____

Just a Note...
_____
_____
_____
_____
_____
_____

Barbecue-glazed Drumsticks

SERVES 6

INGREDIENTS

- 12 chicken drumsticks
- I cup barbecue sauce
- I tbsp brown sugar
- I tbsp cider vinegar
- I tsp salt
- ½ tsp pepper
- ½ tsp hot sauce
- vegetable oil, for greasing

1 With a sharp knife, make 2 slashes, about I inch/2.5 cm apart, into the thickest part of the drumsticks, cutting to the bone. Transfer the chicken to a large, sealable plastic freezer bag.

2 In a small bowl, mix together ¼ cup of the barbecue sauce with the rest of the ingredients. Pour into the bag of chicken, press out most of the air, and seal tightly. Shake the bag gently to distribute the sauce evenly. Refrigerate for at least 4 hours.

3 Preheat the oven to 400°F/200°C. Line a baking sheet with foil and brush lightly with oil.

4 Remove the chicken from the bag with tongs and space evenly on the prepared sheet. Discard the contents of the bag. Brush both sides of the drumsticks with some of the remaining barbecue sauce.

5 Bake in the preheated oven for 15 minutes, then remove from the oven, and brush generously with more sauce. Return to the oven, and repeat this process 3 more times for a total cooking time of I hour. When done, the chicken will be cooked through with a beautiful thick glaze.

CHILDREN'S FAVORITE

Hints & Tips

Recipe: _____
Serves: _____
Ingredients: _____
_____
_____
_____
_____
_____

Method:
_____
_____
_____
_____
_____
_____
_____
_____
_____

Recipe: _____
Serves: _____
Ingredients: _____
_____
_____
_____
_____
_____

Method:
_____
_____
_____
_____
_____
_____
_____
_____
_____

Just a Note...
_____
_____
_____
_____
_____
_____
_____

Just a Note...
_____
_____
_____
_____
_____
_____
_____

Potato Pancakes

MAKES 12 PANCAKES

INGREDIENTS

- 4 large potatoes, peeled and coarsely grated
- 1 large onion, grated
- 2 extra-large eggs, lightly beaten
- ⅓ cup fine matzo meal
- 1 tsp salt
- pepper
- sunflower oil, for frying

TO SERVE

- sour cream
- thinly sliced smoked salmon
- snipped chives

1 Preheat the oven to low and line a heatproof plate with paper towels. Working in small batches, put the potatoes on a dish towel, then gather up the edges of the dish towel and squeeze to extract as much water as possible.

2 Put the potatoes in a large bowl, add the onion, eggs, matzo meal, salt, and pepper to taste, and mix together.

3 Heat a large, heavy-bottom skillet over medium–high heat. Add a thin layer of oil and heat until hot.

4 Drop 2 tablespoons of the batter into the skillet and flatten slightly. Add as many more pancakes as will fit without overcrowding the skillet. Fry for 2 minutes, or until crisp and golden underneath. Flip or turn, using a spatula, and continue frying for an additional 1–2 minutes, until crisp and golden.

5 Repeat this process using the remaining batter. Meanwhile, transfer the cooked pancakes to the prepared plate and keep warm in the preheated oven. Add extra oil to the skillet between batches, if necessary.

6 Serve the pancakes hot, topped with sour cream and smoked salmon, and sprinkled with snipped chives.

IDEAL LIGHT BITE

Popovers

MAKES 6 POPOVERS

INGREDIENTS

- 2 tbsp beef drippings or sunflower oil
- 1 cup all-purpose flour
- ½ tsp salt
- 2 extra-large eggs
- 1 cup milk

1 Grease six metal popover molds or six cups in a muffin pan with the drippings, then divide the remaining drippings between the molds. Preheat the oven to 425°F/220°C, placing the molds in the oven so the drippings can melt while the oven heats.

2 Sift the flour and salt together into a large mixing bowl and make a well in the center. Break the eggs into the well, add the milk, and beat, gradually drawing in the flour from the side to make a smooth batter. Remove the molds from the oven and spoon in the batter until they are about halfway full.

3 Bake in the preheated oven for 30–35 minutes, without opening the door, until the popovers are well risen, puffed, and golden brown. Serve immediately.

COOK'S TIP
Provide each child with a money box to start a savings habit. Let them keep whatever they find on regular coin hunts down the back of the sofa and under furniture.

Hints & Tips

Recipe: _____
Serves: _____
Ingredients: _____
_____
_____
_____
_____

Method: _____
_____
_____
_____
_____
_____
_____
_____
_____

Recipe: _____
Serves: _____
Ingredients: _____
_____
_____
_____
_____

Method: _____
_____
_____
_____
_____
_____
_____
_____
_____

Just a Note...
_____
_____
_____
_____
_____
_____

Just a Note...
_____
_____
_____
_____
_____
_____

Roasted Potatoes

SERVES 6

INGREDIENTS

- 3 lb/1.3 kg large mealy potatoes, peeled and cut into even chunks
- 3 tbsp drippings, goose fat, duck fat, or olive oil
- salt

1 Preheat the oven to 425°F/220°C.

2 Bring a large saucepan of lightly salted water to a boil, add the potatoes, and cook over medium heat, covered, for 5–7 minutes. They will still be firm. Remove from the heat.

3 Meanwhile, add the drippings to a roasting pan and place in the preheated oven.

4 Drain the potatoes well and return them to the pan. Cover with the lid and firmly shake the pan so that the surface of the potatoes is roughened to help give a much crisper texture.

5 Remove the roasting pan from the oven and carefully put the potatoes into the hot fat. Baste them to ensure they are all coated with the fat.

6 Roast at the top of the oven for 45–50 minutes, until they are browned all over and thoroughly crisp. Turn and baste again only once during the cooking process or the crunchy edges will be destroyed.

7 Carefully transfer the potatoes from the roasting pan into a warmed serving dish. Sprinkle with a little salt and serve immediately.

GUILTY PLEASURE

Hints & Tips

Recipe: _____
Serves: _____
Ingredients: _____
_____
_____
_____
_____

Method:
_____
_____
_____
_____
_____
_____
_____
_____
_____
_____

Recipe: _____
Serves: _____
Ingredients: _____
_____
_____
_____
_____

Method: _____
_____
_____
_____
_____
_____
_____
_____
_____

Just a Note...
_____

_____

_____

_____

_____

Just a Note...
_____

_____

_____

_____

_____

Hints & Tips

_____

_____

_____

_____

_____

_____

_____

_____

_____

_____

_____

_____

_____

_____

Recipe: _____

Serves: _____

Ingredients: _____

_____

_____

_____

_____

Method: _____

_____

_____

_____

_____

_____

_____

_____

_____

Recipe: _____

Serves: _____

Ingredients: _____

_____

_____

_____

_____

Method: _____

_____

_____

_____

_____

_____

_____

_____

_____

Just a Note...

_____

_____

_____

_____

_____

_____

Just a Note...

_____

_____

_____

_____

_____

_____

FAMILY
DINNERS

Roasted Chicken

SERVES 6

INGREDIENTS

- 5 lb/2.25 kg chicken
- 4 tbsp butter
- 2 tbsp chopped fresh
  lemon thyme
- 1 lemon, quartered
- ½ cup white wine,
  plus extra if needed
- salt and pepper

1 Preheat the oven to 425°F/220°C.

2 Make sure the chicken is clean, wiping it inside and out using paper towels, and place in a roasting pan.

3 In a bowl, soften the butter with a fork, mix in the thyme, and season well with salt and pepper.

4 Butter the chicken all over with the thyme butter, inside and out, and place the lemon pieces inside the body cavity. Pour the wine over the chicken.

5 Roast in the center of the preheated oven for 20 minutes. Reduce the temperature to 375°F/190°C and continue to roast for an additional 1¼ hours, basting frequently. Cover with foil if the skin begins to brown too much. If the pan dries out, add a little more wine or water.

6 Test that the chicken is cooked by piercing the thickest part of the leg with a sharp knife or skewer. If the juices run clear, the bird is done. Remove from the oven.

7 Remove the chicken from the roasting pan and place on a warmed serving plate, cover with foil, and let rest for 10 minutes before carving.

8 Place the roasting pan on the stove and bubble the pan juices gently over low heat until they have reduced and are thick and glossy. Season with salt and pepper to taste.

9 Serve the chicken with the pan juices.

COOK'S TIP
To give more depth and a touch of sweetness to the finished dish, add a generous splash of Marsala to the pan juices when reducing them.

Hints & Tips

Recipe: _____
Serves: _____
Ingredients: _____
_____
_____
_____
_____

Method: _____
_____
_____
_____
_____
_____
_____
_____
_____
_____
_____

Recipe: _____
Serves: _____
Ingredients: _____
_____
_____
_____
_____

Method: _____
_____
_____
_____
_____
_____
_____
_____
_____
_____
_____

Just a Note...

_____
_____
_____
_____
_____

Just a Note...

_____
_____
_____
_____
_____

Hints & Tips

Recipe: _____
Serves: _____
Ingredients: _____
_____
_____
_____
_____

Method: _____
_____
_____
_____
_____
_____
_____
_____
_____
_____

Recipe: _____
Serves: _____
Ingredients: _____
_____
_____
_____
_____

Method: _____
_____
_____
_____
_____
_____
_____
_____
_____
_____

Just a Note...
_____
_____
_____
_____
_____

Just a Note...
_____
_____
_____
_____
_____

Roasted Rib of Beef

SERVES 8

INGREDIENTS

- olive oil
- 6 lb 8-oz/3-kg joint of well-hung rib of beef on the bone
- ½ tbsp all-purpose flour
- generous ¾ cup strong beef stock
- generous ¾ cup red wine

ROASTED POTATOES

- 4 lb 8 oz/2 kg potatoes, peeled
- 6 tbsp sunflower oil, goose fat, or duck fat
- salt and pepper

TO SERVE

- Popovers (see page 64)
- glazed carrots
- steamed broccoli
- horseradish sauce
- mustard

1 To make the roasted potatoes, bring a large saucepan of lightly salted water to a boil, add the potatoes, return to a boil, and cook for 10 minutes. Drain the potatoes and toss them in oil and salt and pepper. Put them in a roasting pan in a single layer.

2 Preheat the oven to 425°F/220°C. Rub a generous amount of oil and salt and pepper into the beef, then place in a separate roasting pan. Transfer to the preheated oven and roast for 30 minutes.

3 Reduce the oven temperature to 325°F/160°C. Transfer the potatoes to the oven and roast with the beef for 60 minutes. Remove the beef from the oven and increase the temperature to 425°F/220°C. Transfer the beef to a warmed platter, cover with foil, and let rest for at least 30 minutes.

4 Meanwhile, make the gravy. Stir the flour into the leftover juices in the pan, add the stock and wine, then simmer over medium heat, until reduced by about half.

5 Remove the potatoes from the oven. Cut the rib bones off the beef and carve the meat. Serve with the potatoes, popovers, carrots, broccoli, horseradish sauce, and mustard.

HEART WARMING FOOD

Hints & Tips

Recipe: _____
Serves: _____
Ingredients: _____
_____
_____
_____
_____

Method:
_____
_____
_____
_____
_____
_____
_____
_____
_____

Recipe: _____
Serves: _____
Ingredients: _____
_____
_____
_____
_____

Method:
_____
_____
_____
_____
_____
_____
_____
_____
_____

Just a Note...
_____
_____
_____
_____
_____
_____

Just a Note...
_____
_____
_____
_____
_____
_____

Meatloaf

SERVES 6–8

INGREDIENTS

- 3 garlic cloves, peeled
- ½ cup diced carrot
- ½ cup diced celery
- ½ cup diced yellow onion
- ½ cup diced red bell pepper
- 4 large white
  mushrooms, sliced
- 2 tbsp butter
- 1 tbsp olive oil, plus extra
  for greasing
- 1 tsp dried thyme
- 2 tsp finely chopped
  fresh rosemary
- 1 tsp Worcestershire sauce
- ¼ cup ketchup
- ½ tsp cayenne pepper
- 2 lb 8 oz/1.2 kg ground
  chuck steak, well chilled
- 2 tsp salt
- 1 tsp pepper
- 2 eggs, beaten
- 1 cup plain breadcrumbs
- mashed potatoes and peas,
  to serve

GLAZE

- 2 tbsp brown sugar
- 2 tbsp ketchup
- 1 tbsp Dijon mustard
- pinch of salt

1 Put the garlic, carrot, celery, onion, bell pepper, and mushrooms into a food processor. Blend on and off until the vegetables are very finely minced (several times during the processing, scrape down the sides of the bowl with a spatula so the vegetables mince evenly).

2 Add the butter and oil to a large skillet and heat over medium heat. Add the vegetable mixture and cook, stirring, for about 10 minutes, until most of the excess moisture has evaporated and the mixture is lightly caramelized.

3 Remove from the heat and stir in the thyme, rosemary, Worcestershire sauce, ketchup, and cayenne pepper. Set aside and let cool to room temperature.

4 Preheat the oven to 325°F/160°C. Put the meat into a large mixing bowl and very gently break it up with your fingertips. Pour in the cooled vegetable mixture, salt, pepper, and eggs. Gently combine with your fingertips for just 30 seconds. Add the breadcrumbs and continue mixing until combined. The less you work the meat, the better the texture of the meatloaf.

5 Lightly grease a shallow roasting pan with oil. Place the meatloaf mixture in the center of the pan. Wet your hands with cold water and form into a loaf shape about 6 inches/15 cm wide and 4 inches/10 cm high. Wet your hands again and smooth the surface. Place in the center of the preheated oven and cook for 30 minutes.

6 Meanwhile, make the glaze. Whisk all the ingredients together in a small bowl. Remove the meatloaf from the oven and spread the glaze evenly over the top with a spoon. Spread some glaze down the sides as well.

7 Return to the oven and continue baking for 35–45 minutes, or until the internal temperature reaches 155°F/70°C. Remove and let rest for at least 15 minutes before slicing and serving, accompanied by mashed potatoes and peas.

Hints & Tips

Recipe: _____
Serves: _____
Ingredients: _____
_____
_____
_____
_____

Method:
_____
_____
_____
_____
_____
_____
_____
_____

Recipe: _____
Serves: _____
Ingredients: _____
_____
_____
_____
_____

Method:
_____
_____
_____
_____
_____
_____
_____

Just a Note...
_____
_____
_____
_____
_____
_____

Just a Note...
_____
_____
_____
_____
_____
_____

Poached Salmon

SERVES 6

INGREDIENTS

- 6–8 lb/2.7–3.6 kg salmon (head on)
- 3 tbsp salt
- 3 bay leaves
- 10 peppercorns
- 1 onion, peeled and sliced
- 1 lemon, sliced
- lemon wedges, to serve

1 Wipe the salmon thoroughly inside and out with paper towels, then use the back of a cook's knife to remove any scales that might still be on the skin. Remove the fins with a pair of scissors and trim the tail. Some people prefer to remove the head but it is traditionally served with it on.

2 Place the salmon on a two-handled rack and place in a fish poacher. Fill the poacher with enough cold water to cover the salmon adequately. Sprinkle in the salt, bay leaves, and peppercorns and add the onion and lemon slices.

3 Place over two low burners and very slowly bring just to a boil.

4 Cover and simmer very gently. To serve cold, simmer for only 2 minutes, remove from the heat, and cool in the cooking water for about 2 hours with the lid on. To serve hot, simmer for 6–8 minutes and let the fish stand in the hot water for 15 minutes before removing. Serve with lemon wedges for squeezing over.

IMPRESS THE FAMILY

Hints & Tips

Recipe: _____
Serves: _____
Ingredients: _____
_____
_____
_____
_____

Method: _____
_____
_____
_____
_____
_____
_____
_____
_____
_____

Recipe: _____
Serves: _____
Ingredients: _____
_____
_____
_____
_____

Method: _____
_____
_____
_____
_____
_____
_____
_____
_____
_____

Just a Note...
_____
_____
_____
_____
_____

Just a Note...
_____
_____
_____
_____
_____

Hints & Tips

_____

_____

_____

_____

_____

_____

_____

_____

_____

_____

_____

_____

_____

_____

Recipe: _____
Serves: _____
Ingredients: _____
_____
_____
_____
_____

Method: _____
_____
_____
_____
_____
_____
_____
_____
_____
_____

Recipe: _____
Serves: _____
Ingredients: _____
_____
_____
_____
_____

Method: _____
_____
_____
_____
_____
_____
_____
_____
_____
_____

Just a Note...

_____
_____
_____
_____
_____

Just a Note...

_____
_____
_____
_____
_____

Asparagus & Tomato Quiche

SERVES 4

INGREDIENTS

- butter, for greasing
- 13 oz/375 g prepared pastry
- 1 bunch of thin
  asparagus spears
- 9 oz/250 g spinach leaves
- 3 extra-large eggs, beaten
- ⅔ cup heavy cream
- 1 garlic clove, crushed
- 10 small cherry
  tomatoes, halved
- handful of fresh basil,
  chopped
- ¼ cup grated
  Parmesan cheese
- salt and pepper

1 Preheat the oven to 375°F/190°C. Grease a 10–12-inch/25–30-cm tart pan with butter, then roll out the pastry and line the pan with it.

2 Cut off any excess, prick the bottom with a fork, cover with a piece of wax paper, and fill with dried beans, then bake in the preheated oven for 20–30 minutes, until lightly browned. Remove from the oven and let cool slightly. Reduce the oven temperature to 350°F/180°C.

3 Meanwhile, bend the asparagus spears until they snap, and discard the woody ends. Bring a large saucepan of water to a boil, add the asparagus, and blanch for 1 minute, then remove and drain. Add the spinach to the boiling water, then remove and drain very well.

4 Mix the eggs, cream, and garlic together and season with salt and pepper to taste. Lay the blanched spinach at the bottom of the pastry shell, add the asparagus and tomatoes, cut-side up, in any arrangement you like, scatter over the basil, then pour the egg mixture on top.

5 Transfer to the oven and bake for about 35 minutes, or until the filling has set. Sprinkle over the Parmesan cheese and let cool to room temperature before serving.

COOK'S TIP
This is a great dish to make for summer picnics and outdoor parties. The ingredients are interchangeable with other crisp spring and summer vegetables.

Hints & Tips

Recipe: _____
Serves: _____
Ingredients: _____
_____
_____
_____
_____

Method: _____
_____
_____
_____
_____
_____
_____
_____
_____

Recipe: _____
Serves: _____
Ingredients: _____
_____
_____
_____
_____

Method: _____
_____
_____
_____
_____
_____
_____
_____
_____

Just a Note...
_____
_____
_____
_____
_____
_____
_____

Just a Note...
_____
_____
_____
_____
_____
_____
_____

Hints & Tips

_____
_____
_____
_____
_____
_____
_____
_____
_____
_____
_____
_____
_____

Recipe: _____
Serves: _____
Ingredients: _____
_____
_____
_____
_____

Method: _____
_____
_____
_____
_____
_____
_____
_____
_____

Recipe: _____
Serves: _____
Ingredients: _____
_____
_____
_____
_____

Method: _____
_____
_____
_____
_____
_____
_____
_____
_____

Just a Note...

_____

_____

_____

_____

_____

Just a Note...

_____

_____

_____

_____

_____

Hints & Tips

Recipe: _____
Serves: _____
Ingredients: _____
_____
_____
_____
_____

Method: _____
_____
_____
_____
_____
_____
_____
_____
_____

Recipe: _____
Serves: _____
Ingredients: _____
_____
_____
_____
_____

Method: _____
_____
_____
_____
_____
_____
_____
_____
_____

Just a Note...
_____
_____
_____
_____
_____
_____

Just a Note...
_____
_____
_____
_____
_____
_____

BAKING
DAY

Raspberry Sponge Cake

SERVES 8–10

INGREDIENTS

- ¾ cup unsalted butter, at room temperature, plus extra for greasing
- ¾ cup superfine sugar
- 3 eggs, beaten
- scant 1½ cups self-rising flour
- pinch of salt
- 3 tbsp raspberry jelly
- confectioners' sugar, for dusting

1 Preheat the oven to 350°F/180°C.

2 Grease two 8-inch/20-cm round cake pans and line with parchment paper.

3 Cream the butter and sugar together in a mixing bowl using a wooden spoon or a handheld mixer, until the mixture is pale in color and light and fluffy.

4 Add the eggs, one at a time, beating well after each addition.

5 Sift the flour and salt together into a separate bowl and carefully add to the mixture, folding it in with a metal spoon or a spatula. Divide the mixture between the prepared pans, smoothing the surface.

6 Place the pans in the center of the preheated oven and bake for 25–30 minutes, until the cakes are well risen, golden brown, and beginning to shrink from the sides of the pans.

7 Remove from the oven and let stand for 1 minute.

8 Loosen the cakes from around the edge of the pans using a palette knife. Turn out onto a clean dish towel, remove the paper, and invert the cakes onto a wire rack (this prevents the wire rack from marking the top of the cakes).

9 When completely cool, sandwich the cakes together with the jelly and dust with confectioners' sugar. The cake is delicious when freshly baked, but any remaining cake can be stored in an airtight container for up to 1 week.

FEEL-BETTER FOOD

Hints & Tips

_____

_____

_____

_____

_____

_____

_____

_____

_____

_____

_____

_____

_____

_____

Recipe: _____
Serves: _____
Ingredients: _____
_____
_____
_____
_____

Method: _____
_____
_____
_____
_____
_____
_____
_____

Recipe: _____
Serves: _____
Ingredients: _____
_____
_____
_____
_____

Method: _____
_____
_____
_____
_____
_____
_____
_____
_____
_____

Just a Note...
_____
_____
_____
_____
_____

Just a Note...
_____
_____
_____
_____
_____

Apple Pie

SERVES 6

INGREDIENTS

PIE DOUGH

- 2½ cups all-purpose flour, plus extra for dusting
- pinch of salt
- 6 tbsp butter, cut into small pieces, plus extra for greasing
- 6 tbsp lard or vegetable shortening, cut into small pieces
- about 6 tbsp cold water
- beaten egg or milk, for glazing

FILLING

- 1 lb 10 oz–2 lb 4 oz/ 750 g–1 kg baking apples, peeled, cored, and sliced
- scant ⅔ cup brown or superfine sugar, plus extra for sprinkling
- ½–1 tsp ground cinnamon, allspice, or ground ginger
- 1–2 tbsp water (optional)

1 To make the pie dough, sift together the flour and salt into a large bowl. Add the butter and lard and rub in with your fingertips until the mixture resembles fine breadcrumbs. Add the water and gather the mixture together into a dough. Wrap the dough and let chill in the refrigerator for 30 minutes.

2 Preheat the oven to 425°F/220°C. Turn out almost two-thirds of the pie dough onto a floured counter, roll out thinly, and use to line a deep 9-inch/ 23-cm pie plate or pie pan.

3 To make the filling, mix the apples with the sugar and spice and pack into the pastry shell. Add the water, if needed, particularly if the apples are a dry variety.

4 Roll out the remaining pie dough to form a lid. Dampen the edges of the pie rim with water and position the lid, pressing the edges firmly together. Trim and crimp the edges.

5 Use the trimmings to cut out leaves or other shapes to decorate the top of the pie. Dampen and attach. Glaze the top of the pie with beaten egg, make 1–2 slits in the top, and place the pie on a baking sheet.

6 Bake in the preheated oven for 20 minutes, then reduce the oven temperature to 350°F/180°C and bake for an additional 30 minutes, or until the pastry is golden brown. Serve hot or cold, sprinkled with sugar.

COOK'S TIP
Prevent apples from discoloring by placing the peeled slices in a bowl of water with the juice of 1 lemon added.

Hints & Tips

Recipe: _____
Serves: _____
Ingredients: _____
_____
_____
_____
_____

Method: _____
_____
_____
_____
_____
_____
_____
_____
_____

Recipe: _____
Serves: _____
Ingredients: _____
_____
_____
_____
_____

Method: _____
_____
_____
_____
_____
_____
_____
_____
_____

Just a Note...
_____
_____
_____
_____
_____
_____

Just a Note...
_____
_____
_____
_____
_____
_____

Blueberry Crumb Cake

SERVES 12

INGREDIENTS

- 2 cups fresh blueberries
- 3 cups self-rising flour, plus extra for dusting
- 1¼ tsp salt
- ½ tsp apple pie spice
- 1¼ cups butter, at room temperature, plus extra for greasing
- 1¾ cups superfine sugar
- ½ tsp vanilla extract
- ½ tsp almond extract
- 2 extra-large eggs
- 1¼–1½ cups sour cream

ALMOND STREUSEL TOPPING

- ½ cup butter, diced
- 1 cup all-purpose flour
- 2 tbsp light brown sugar
- 1 tbsp granulated sugar
- generous ¼ cup chopped blanched almonds

1 To make the almond streusel topping, put the butter and flour into a large bowl and rub together until coarse crumbs form. Stir in both types of sugar and the almonds, then let chill in the refrigerator until required.

2 Preheat the oven to 350°F/180°C. Butter a 13 × 9-inch/ 33 × 23-cm rectangular cake pan and dust with flour. Dust the blueberries with 1 tablespoon of the measured flour and set aside. Sift the remaining flour into a bowl with the salt and apple pie spice and set aside.

3 Place the butter in a large bowl and, using an electric mixer, beat until soft and creamy. Add the sugar, vanilla extract, and almond extract and continue beating until the mixture is light and fluffy. Add the eggs,

one at a time, beating well after each addition, then beat in 1¼ cups of the sour cream. Beat in the flour until the mixture is soft and falls easily from a spoon. Add the remaining sour cream, 1 tablespoon at a time, if necessary.

4 Add the blueberries and any loose flour to the batter and quickly fold in. Pour the batter into the prepared pan and smooth the surface. Pinch the topping into large crumbs and scatter evenly over the batter.

5 Bake the cake in the preheated oven for 45–55 minutes, until it comes away from the side of the pan and a toothpick inserted in the center comes out clean. Transfer the pan to a wire rack and let the cake cool completely. Cut into 12 slices and serve straight from the pan.

COOK'S TIP
When a recipe says "dot with butter," shave off curls from a cold stick with a vegetable peeler.

Hints & Tips

Recipe: _____
Serves: _____
Ingredients: _____
_____
_____
_____
_____

Method: _____
_____
_____
_____
_____
_____
_____
_____
_____
_____

Recipe: _____
Serves: _____
Ingredients: _____
_____
_____
_____
_____

Method: _____
_____
_____
_____
_____
_____
_____
_____
_____
_____

Just a Note...

_____

_____

_____

_____

_____

Just a Note...

_____

_____

_____

_____

_____

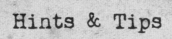

Hints & Tips

Recipe: _____
Serves: _____
Ingredients: _____
_____
_____
_____
_____
_____

Method: _____
_____
_____
_____
_____
_____
_____
_____
_____

Recipe: _____
Serves: _____
Ingredients: _____
_____
_____
_____
_____
_____

Method: _____
_____
_____
_____
_____
_____
_____
_____
_____

Just a Note...
_____
_____
_____
_____
_____
_____

Just a Note...
_____
_____
_____
_____
_____
_____

Mega Chip Cookies

MAKES 12 LARGE COOKIES

INGREDIENTS

- 1 cup butter, softened
- scant ¾ cup superfine sugar
- 1 egg yolk, lightly beaten
- 2 tsp vanilla extract
- 2 cups all-purpose flour
- ½ cup unsweetened cocoa
- pinch of salt
- ½ cup milk chocolate chips
- ½ cup white chocolate chips
- 4 oz/115 g bittersweet chocolate, coarsely chopped

1 Preheat the oven to 375°F/190°C. Line 2–3 cookie sheets with baking parchment.

2 Put the butter and sugar into a bowl and mix well with a wooden spoon, then beat in the egg yolk and vanilla extract. Sift the flour, cocoa, and salt together into the mixture, add both kinds of chocolate chips, and stir until thoroughly combined.

3 Make 12 balls of the mixture, put them on the prepared cookie sheets, spaced well apart, and flatten slightly. Press the pieces of bittersweet chocolate into the cookies.

4 Bake for 12–15 minutes. Let cool on the cookie sheets for 5–10 minutes, then, using a metal spatula, carefully transfer to wire racks to cool completely.

CHILDREN'S FAVORITE

Cinnamon Swirls

MAKES 12 SWIRLS

INGREDIENTS

- 1⅔ cups white bread flour
- ½ tsp salt
- ¼ oz/10 g active dry yeast
- 2 tbsp butter, cut into small pieces, plus extra for greasing
- 1 egg, lightly beaten
- ½ cup lukewarm milk
- 2 tbsp maple syrup, for glazing

FILLING

- 4 tbsp butter, softened
- 2 tsp ground cinnamon
- ¼ cup light brown sugar
- ⅓ cup currants

1 Grease a baking sheet with a little butter.

2 Sift together the flour and salt into a mixing bowl. Stir in the yeast. Rub in the butter with your fingertips until the mixture resembles breadcrumbs. Add the egg and milk and mix to form a dough.

3 Form the dough into a ball, place in a greased bowl, cover, and let stand in a warm place for about 40 minutes, or until doubled in size.

4 Punch down the dough lightly for 1 minute, then roll out to a rectangle measuring 12 × 9 inches/ 30 × 23 cm.

5 To make the filling, cream together the butter, cinnamon, and brown sugar until light and fluffy. Spread the filling evenly over the dough rectangle, leaving a 1-inch/2.5-cm border all around. Sprinkle the currants evenly over the top.

6 Roll up the dough from one of the long edges, and press down to seal. Cut the roll into 12 slices. Place them, cut-side down, on the baking sheet, cover, and let stand for 30 minutes.

7 Meanwhile, preheat the oven to 375°F/ 190°C. Bake the swirls in the preheated oven for 20–30 minutes, or until well risen. Brush with the maple syrup and let cool slightly before serving.

Hints & Tips

_____

_____

_____

_____

_____

_____

_____

_____

_____

_____

_____

_____

_____

_____

_____

Recipe: _____
Serves: _____
Ingredients: _____
_____
_____
_____
_____

Method: _____
_____
_____
_____
_____
_____
_____
_____
_____

Recipe: _____
Serves: _____
Ingredients: _____
_____
_____
_____
_____

Method: _____
_____
_____
_____
_____
_____
_____
_____
_____

Just a Note...
_____
_____
_____
_____
_____

Just a Note...
_____
_____
_____
_____
_____

Hints & Tips

Recipe: _____
Serves: _____
Ingredients: _____

_____
_____
_____

Method: _____

_____
_____
_____
_____
_____
_____
_____

Recipe: _____
Serves: _____
Ingredients: _____

_____
_____
_____

Method: _____

_____
_____
_____
_____
_____
_____
_____

Just a Note...

_____
_____
_____
_____
_____

Just a Note...

_____
_____
_____
_____
_____

Hints & Tips

Recipe: _____
Serves: _____
Ingredients: _____
_____
_____
_____
_____

Method: _____
_____
_____
_____
_____
_____
_____
_____
_____

Recipe: _____
Serves: _____
Ingredients: _____
_____
_____
_____
_____

Method: _____
_____
_____
_____
_____
_____
_____
_____
_____

Just a Note...
_____
_____
_____
_____
_____
_____
_____

Just a Note...
_____
_____
_____
_____
_____
_____
_____

Hints & Tips

Recipe: _____
Serves: _____
Ingredients: _____
_____
_____
_____
_____
_____

Method: _____
_____
_____
_____
_____
_____
_____
_____
_____

Recipe: _____
Serves: _____
Ingredients: _____
_____
_____
_____
_____
_____

Method: _____
_____
_____
_____
_____
_____
_____
_____
_____

Just a Note...
_____
_____
_____
_____
_____

Just a Note...
_____
_____
_____
_____
_____

Cornbread

MAKES 1 SMALL LOAF

INGREDIENTS

- vegetable oil, for brushing
- 1½ cups all-purpose flour
- 1 tsp salt
- 4 tsp baking powder
- 1 tsp superfine sugar
- 2½ cups yellow cornmeal
- ¾ cup butter, softened
- 4 eggs
- 1 cup milk
- 3 tbsp heavy cream

1 Preheat the oven to 400°F/200°C. Brush an 8-inch/20-cm square cake pan with oil.

2 Sift together the flour, salt, and baking powder into a bowl. Add the sugar and cornmeal and stir to mix. Add the butter and cut it into the dry ingredients with a knife, then rub in with your fingertips until the mixture resembles fine breadcrumbs.

3 Lightly beat the eggs with the milk and cream in a bowl, then stir into the cornmeal mixture until thoroughly combined.

4 Spoon the mixture into the prepared pan and smooth the surface. Bake for 30–35 minutes, until a toothpick inserted into the center of the loaf comes out clean. Remove the pan from the oven and let the bread cool for 5–10 minutes, then cut into squares and serve warm.

PRACTICE MAKES PERFECT

Hints & Tips

_____

_____

_____

_____

_____

_____

_____

_____

_____

_____

_____

_____

_____

_____

Recipe: _____
Serves: _____
Ingredients: _____
_____
_____
_____
_____

Method: _____
_____
_____
_____
_____
_____
_____
_____
_____

Recipe: _____
Serves: _____
Ingredients: _____
_____
_____
_____
_____

Method: _____
_____
_____
_____
_____
_____
_____
_____
_____

Just a Note...

_____

_____

_____

_____

_____

Just a Note...

_____

_____

_____

_____

_____

Rhubarb Crumble

SERVES 6

INGREDIENTS

- 2 lb/900 g rhubarb
- ½ cup superfine sugar
- grated rind and juice of 1 orange
- custard, to serve

CRUMBLE TOPPING

- scant 1¾ cups all-purpose or whole wheat flour
- ½ cup unsalted butter, diced and chilled
- ½ cup light brown sugar
- 1 tsp ground ginger

1 Preheat the oven to 375°F/190°C.

2 Cut the rhubarb into 1-inch/2.5-cm lengths and put in an ovenproof dish with the sugar and the orange rind and juice.

3 To make the crumble topping, sift the flour into a bowl. Rub in the butter with your fingertips until the mixture resembles fine breadcrumbs. Stir in the sugar and ginger.

4 Spread the crumble topping evenly over the fruit and press down lightly with a fork.

5 Bake in the center of the preheated oven for 25–30 minutes, until the crumble is golden brown. Serve warm with custard.

COOK'S TIP
Use very young shoots of rhubarb because they are the sweetest. A handful of strawberries would be a good addition, since they enhance the flavor and color.

Hints & Tips

Recipe: _____
Serves: _____
Ingredients: _____
_____
_____
_____
_____

Method: _____
_____
_____
_____
_____
_____
_____
_____

Recipe: _____
Serves: _____
Ingredients: _____
_____
_____
_____
_____

Method: _____
_____
_____
_____
_____
_____
_____
_____

Just a Note...

_____

_____

_____

_____

_____

Just a Note...

_____

_____

_____

_____

_____

Banana Cream Pie

SERVES 8–10

INGREDIENTS

- ¼ cup all-purpose flour, for dusting
- 12 oz/350 g prepared pastry, thawed, if frozen
- 4 extra-large egg yolks
- heaped ¾ cup superfine sugar
- 4 tbsp cornstarch
- pinch of salt
- 2 cups milk
- 1 tsp vanilla extract
- 3 bananas
- ½ tbsp lemon juice
- 1½ cups whipping cream, whipped with 3 tbsp confectioners' sugar, to decorate

1 Preheat the oven to 400°F/200°C. Very lightly flour a rolling pin and use to roll out the dough on a lightly floured counter to a 12-inch/30-cm circle. Line a 9-inch/23-cm pie plate with the dough, then trim the excess dough and prick the bottom all over with a fork. Line the pastry shell with parchment paper and fill with dried beans.

2 Bake in the preheated oven for 15 minutes, or until the pastry is a light golden color. Remove the paper and beans and prick the bottom again. Return to the oven and bake for an additional 5–10 minutes, until golden and dry. Transfer to a wire rack and let cool completely.

3 Meanwhile, put the egg yolks, sugar, cornstarch, and salt into a bowl and beat until blended and pale in color. Beat in the milk and vanilla extract.

4 Pour the mixture into a heavy-bottom saucepan set over medium–high heat and bring to a boil, stirring, until smooth and thick. Reduce the heat to low and simmer, stirring, for 2 minutes. Strain the mixture into a bowl and set aside to cool.

5 Slice the bananas, place in a bowl with the lemon juice, and toss. Arrange them in the cooled pastry shell, then top with the custard and let chill in the refrigerator for at least 2 hours. Spread the whipped cream over the top and serve immediately.

COOK'S TIP
Old-fashioned metal pie plates, cake pans, and tart pans conduct heat better than glass, earthenware, or porcelain, producing even baking and reducing the cooking time.

New York Cheesecake

SERVES 10

INGREDIENTS

- generous ½ cup butter, plus extra for greasing
- 1½ cups finely crushed graham crackers
- 1 tbsp granulated sugar
- 4 cups cream cheese
- 1¼ cups superfine sugar
- 2 tbsp all-purpose flour
- 1 tsp vanilla extract
- finely grated zest of 1 orange
- finely grated zest of 1 lemon
- 3 eggs
- 2 egg yolks
- 1½ cups heavy cream

1 Preheat the oven to 350°F/180°C. Place a small saucepan over low heat, add the butter, and heat until melted, then remove from the heat, stir in the crackers and granulated sugar, and mix through.

2 Press the cracker mixture tightly into the bottom of a 9-inch/23-cm springform cake pan. Place in the oven and bake for 10 minutes. Remove from the oven and let cool on a wire rack.

3 Increase the oven temperature to 400°F/200°C. With an electric mixer beat the cheese until creamy, then gradually add the superfine sugar and flour and beat until smooth. Increase the speed and beat in the vanilla extract, orange zest, and lemon zest, then beat in the eggs and egg yolks one at a time. Finally, beat in the cream. Scrape any excess into the mixture. It should be light and whippy—beat on a faster setting if you need to.

4 Butter the side of the cake pan and pour in the filling. Smooth the top, transfer to the preheated oven, and bake for 15 minutes, then reduce the temperature to 225°F/110°C and bake for an additional 30 minutes. Turn off the oven and let the cheesecake stand in it for 2 hours to cool and set. Cover and refrigerate overnight.

5 Slide a knife around the edge of the cake, then unfasten the pan, cut the cheesecake into wedge-shape slices, and serve.

GUILTY PLEASURE

Hints & Tips

_____

_____

_____

_____

_____

_____

_____

_____

_____

_____

_____

_____

_____

_____

Recipe: _____

Serves: _____

Ingredients: _____
_____
_____
_____
_____

Method: _____
_____
_____
_____
_____
_____
_____
_____
_____
_____

Recipe: _____

Serves: _____

Ingredients: _____
_____
_____
_____
_____

Method: _____
_____
_____
_____
_____
_____
_____
_____
_____
_____

Just a Note...
_____
_____
_____
_____
_____
_____

Just a Note...
_____
_____
_____
_____
_____
_____

Hints & Tips

_____

_____

_____

_____

_____

_____

_____

_____

_____

_____

_____

_____

_____

Recipe: _____

Serves: _____

Ingredients: _____
_____
_____
_____
_____

Method: _____
_____
_____
_____
_____
_____
_____
_____
_____

Recipe: _____

Serves: _____

Ingredients: _____
_____
_____
_____
_____

Method: _____
_____
_____
_____
_____
_____
_____
_____
_____

Just a Note...
_____
_____
_____
_____
_____
_____

Just a Note...
_____
_____
_____
_____
_____
_____

Bread & Butter Pudding

SERVES 4–6

INGREDIENTS

- 6 tbsp butter, softened
- 6 slices thick white bread
- ⅓ cup mixed dried fruit
- 2 tbsp candied peel
- 3 extra-large eggs
- 1¼ cups milk
- ⅔ cup heavy cream
- ¼ cup superfine sugar
- whole nutmeg, for grating
- 1 tbsp raw sugar
- heavy cream, to serve

1 Preheat the oven to 350°F/180°C.

2 Use a little of the butter to grease an 8 × 10-inch/20 × 25-cm baking dish and butter the slices of bread. Cut the bread into quarters and arrange half overlapping in the dish.

3 Scatter half of the dried fruit and peel over the bread, cover with the remaining bread slices, and add the remaining fruit and peel.

4 In a pitcher, whisk the eggs well and mix in the milk, cream, and sugar. Pour this over the pudding and let stand for 15 minutes to let the bread soak up some of the egg mixture. Tuck in most of the fruit so it doesn't burn in the oven.

5 Grate nutmeg over the top of the pudding to taste, and sprinkle over the raw sugar.

6 Place the dessert on a baking sheet and bake in the top of the oven for 30–40 minutes, until just set and golden brown.

7 Remove from the oven and serve warm with a little cream.

COOK'S TIP
Try using brioche or a lightly fruited loaf instead of white bread. Any mixture of dried fruit can be used, so why not experiment with your favorites?

Hints & Tips

Recipe: _____
Serves: _____
Ingredients: _____
_____
_____
_____
_____

Method: _____
_____
_____
_____
_____
_____
_____
_____
_____
_____

Recipe: _____
Serves: _____
Ingredients: _____
_____
_____
_____
_____

Method: _____
_____
_____
_____
_____
_____
_____
_____
_____
_____

Just a Note...
_____
_____
_____
_____
_____

Just a Note...
_____
_____
_____
_____
_____

Hints & Tips

_____

_____

_____

_____

_____

_____

_____

_____

_____

_____

_____

_____

_____

_____

Recipe: _____
Serves: _____
Ingredients: _____
_____
_____
_____
_____

Method: _____
_____
_____
_____
_____
_____
_____
_____
_____

Recipe: _____
Serves: _____
Ingredients: _____
_____
_____
_____
_____

Method: _____
_____
_____
_____
_____
_____
_____
_____
_____

Just a Note...
_____
_____
_____
_____
_____
_____

Just a Note...
_____
_____
_____
_____
_____
_____

Hints & Tips

_____

_____

_____

_____

_____

_____

_____

_____

_____

_____

_____

_____

_____

Recipe: _____
Serves: _____
Ingredients: _____
_____
_____
_____
_____

Method: _____
_____
_____
_____
_____
_____
_____
_____
_____

Recipe: _____
Serves: _____
Ingredients: _____
_____
_____
_____
_____

Method: _____
_____
_____
_____
_____
_____
_____
_____
_____

Just a Note...

_____

_____

_____

_____

_____

Just a Note...

_____

_____

_____

_____

_____

Chocolate Fudge

MAKES 32 PIECES

INGREDIENTS

- 2 tbsp unsweetened cocoa
- 1¼ cups milk
- 4½ oz/125 g bittersweet chocolate, at least 85% cocoa solids, finely chopped
- 4 cups superfine sugar
- ½ cup butter, chopped, plus extra for greasing
- pinch of salt
- 1½ tsp vanilla extract
- 1¾ cups pecans, walnuts, or toasted hazelnuts, or a mixture of nuts, chopped

1 Put the cocoa into a small bowl, add 2 tablespoons of the milk, and stir until blended. Pour the remaining milk into a large, heavy-bottom saucepan, then add the cocoa mixture and chocolate and simmer over medium–high heat, stirring, until the chocolate melts. Add the sugar, butter, and salt, reduce the heat to low, and stir until the butter is melted, the sugar is dissolved, and you can't feel any of the grains when you rub a spoon against the side of the pan.

2 Increase the heat and bring the liquid fudge to a boil. Cover the pan and boil for 2 minutes, then uncover and carefully clip a candy thermometer to the side. Continue boiling, without stirring, until the temperature reaches 247°F/115°C, or until a small amount of the mixture forms a soft ball when dropped in cold water.

3 Meanwhile, line an 8-inch/20-cm square cake pan with foil, grease the foil, and set aside.

4 Remove the saucepan from the heat, stir in the vanilla extract, and beat the fudge until it thickens. Stir in the nuts.

5 Pour the fudge mixture into the prepared pan and use a wet spatula to smooth the surface. Set aside and let stand for at least 2 hours to become firm. Lift the fudge out of the pan, then peel off the foil. Cut the fudge into eight 1-inch/2.5-cm strips, then cut each strip into four pieces. Store the fudge for up to 1 week in an airtight container.

fond memories xx